Overcoming
the
Obstacles

By: Donna K. Davis

PRESS

Overcoming the Obstacles
by Donna K. Davis

Printed in the United States of America

ISBN 9781625097750

Unless otherwise indicated, Bible quotations are taken from the New International Version (NIV). Copyright © 2011 by Biblica, Inc.

www.xulonpress.com

Dedication

This book is dedicated to the family and friends who have walked the path of life with me.... hand-in-hand and heart-to-heart. Some of you have been on this journey with me longer than others and have experienced many of the challenges shared within this writing. With your faithful love, encouragement, guidance, support and prayers I have overcome the obstacles by God's grace. Because God chose to use you and bring you into my life I will forever be eternally grateful.

Contents

Introduction

*L*ife is never predictable. Just as seasons change, so does life. It ebbs and flows with glorious events that we want to share with anyone who will lend us an ear all the way down to the "rock bottom" times where we do not know which way to turn. It is during those times that we feel like we have to look up to see the bottom. We all have them. No one is immune from difficulty; it is a part of life. Difficulties, challenges, troubles, and obstacles are no respecter of age, color, race, income, title, or belief. They will come. The question is, do we allow them to direct us or define us? We can see them as an obstacle or an opportunity. We can overcome them or, we can be overcome by them. The choice is ours. God's word says, "The righteous person may have many troubles, BUT the Lord delivers Him from them all" (Psalm 34:19).

In the process of doing life, we will all have "obstacles" and difficulties that cross our path. These are times that provide the opportunity to teach us about life; however, it is not a place we desire to stay for any length of time. As a Christian, these difficulties should bring growth and build faith that cannot be accomplished any other way. When we come through the difficulty or obstacle, we can look back and see what God was trying to do in our lives and later help others who are going through the same or similar struggle.

In the pages of this book I will tell the story of my pursuit of God and His faithfulness to me. What I hope you capture from your reading is this; God is faithful and He can be trusted in all things, at all times, and in all circumstances. Through sharing with you the various bits and pieces of my life, it is my desire to point you to a God who is able to do exceedingly and abundantly above all you are able to ask or think of Him, and ultimately give Him the glory for it all...the good and the bad.

This book is a result of a lifetime of experiences that at times would seem to overtake me, but through the grace of God I stand as a testimony to His faithfulness. About ten years ago, while walking down the church hallway, between Sunday school and the morning worship service, I was talking to one of the board members of the church my husband and I were pastoring about a difficulty I had just been through. At the end of the conversation I told him that one day there will be a book about all that I have gone through, and I know what the title of it will be...***Overcoming the Obstacles***. That thought has never left me from the moment the words rolled off my lips. I believe that God birthed that title in my heart over ten years ago and today you hold the completion of a task that God placed upon my heart to accomplish. From that time until this printing I have pondered the what, why, and how of this writing project. I have never seen myself as a writer... but only doing assignments for undergraduate/ graduate coursework and responsibilities that required me to write within my profession.

When God places a plan or dream in our hearts, it is hard to get away from it. We can drown it out, busy ourselves with other things so that there is no time to complete the task, or just ignore it hoping it will go away, but God is patient and gentle with His promptings. He has a plan and purpose for our lives even if we have never looked at it from that perspective. When we give our life to Jesus Christ and ask Him to be the Lord of our life, it is a daily submission of our will to His. We must be willing to submit all of our plans, purposes, and desires in order for Him to work in our lives. Through our act of yielding and submission, He can use us to do great things for the Kingdom of God.

Many thanks go to my husband of thirty years who has believed in me when I could not believe in myself. Has it been a perfect marriage, oh no, but we have stayed committed to each other when it would have been easier to walk away. The road has not always been easy as we have braved many storms together, but we have a marriage that I know has been a testimony, along the way, to many other couples in and out of ministry. With God at the center of our life and marriage, we have braved the storms that have come our way, and I am sure we will brave many others together.

Thank you to the two beautiful children that God blessed me with and entrusted my husband and me to raise in the fear and admonition of the Lord. All that you will read in the chapters of this book, our two children lived and experienced much of it along with me, watching from the sidelines. A miracle in itself is that God has called both of them into ministry, and I pray that they will always be faithful in fulfilling that call as God directs their steps.

Music has always been a big part of my life. As far back as I can remember I was encouraged to sing in church and use my talents for the Lord. To this day I enjoy being involved in the music ministry of our church and nothing brings me into God's presence more readily than singing praises unto Him. Throughout the book I will share certain worship songs that helped me through difficult times in my life as the words were instrumental in carrying me through to victory.

As I share many of the hardships and obstacles that have crossed my path, I will be an "open book" for you to read. I trust you will not see the author, but a Savior, Jesus Christ, who has a plan for your life just as He has for mine. You may not always understand the way He leads, but you need to become intimately familiar with His character so you can trust Him as He directs the steps of your life. As a Christian, God does not allow anything to come our way that He has not orchestrated for our good. I have not relished the difficult seasons of my life, but I know that God has directed them to draw me closer to Him. The tests have resulted in great testimonies of His faithfulness. May God truly use the contents of this book to make you stronger in your walk and service for His kingdom.

As David wrote in Psalm 66:16-20 of his desire for others to listen as he proclaimed of God's faithfulness unto him; my desire is the same as you read the contents of this book. "Come and hear, all you who fear God; let me tell you what he has done for me. I cried out to him with my mouth; his praise was on my tongue. If I had cherished sin in my heart, the Lord would not have listened; but God has surely listened and has heard my prayer. Praise be to God, who has not rejected my prayer or withheld his love from me!"

~ 1 ~

The Formative Years

"Start children off on the way they should go, and even when they are old they will not turn from it."
Proverbs 22:6

As a young child, I grew up in church; practically on the church pew, as my parents were the right arm of the pastor. Any time the church door was open, we were there. The church we attended had given our pastor's wife a birthday party one Saturday evening and my mom went to the hospital a few hours later to give birth to me the following morning. That is why I have always said, "I was practically born on the church pew" and a Sunday baby at that.

The Christian heritage that was placed in my life, at a young age, set a foundation that I believe sustained me through many difficult times in my life. I am forever grateful to my parents for the heritage and Godly example they lived before me and continue to exemplify to this day. As a result of being born into that Christ-centered atmosphere, I remember God making Himself known to me around the age of four. Eventually I accepted Jesus Christ as my personal Lord and Savior at the age of six during Vacation Bible School. Even at an early age I wanted to know Him in a deeper way.

Growing up in Florida the summers were hot, so I played outside with my siblings and neighbors because there was no air-conditioning in our home. During those times of creative play and cooling off in our tree house, I can remember two occasions where I sensed God making Himself known to me. I knew he was speaking to my heart, assuring me that He was very near and that He desired to be my best friend. That same gentleness of my heavenly Father helped me find my way in the woods, on a camping trip, when I was lost and separated from my family at a very young age. That same nearness kept me when I almost drowned as a young child in a public pool. To this day I do not know how I made it to the side as I was going down for the third time. I ultimately know that God was with me and He had a plan for my life.

My parents always had a heart to serve in ministry and gave of their talents any way they could to see the Kingdom of God advanced. When I was nine years of age they gave up every weekend, for four years, to help start a new church. The church was forty-five miles away from our home, so they purchased a travel trailer and that was home on the weekends for the next four years. They received no compensation; only the satisfaction of knowing that they were helping to change lives and build the Kingdom of God. My mom would get up extra early on Sunday mornings and go pick up immigrant children and bring them to church. Only eternity will reveal the many lives that were touched by the sacrificial love that my parents always demonstrated. I am sure that this sacrificial labor of love that was patterned by my parents left an everlasting mark upon my life. Through their dedication, I learned about living a life of surrender to the will of God and of service to others.

At the age of thirteen, my father left the security of a comfortable salary and accepted a call to serve in full-time ministry as the director of a Christian rehabilitation center for alcoholics. My mother also left her job as a legal secretary and gave of her talents to help in the same ministry that rescued homeless alcoholics from the street. She became the head bookkeeper for the Ft. Lauderdale property and the corporate bookkeeper for the entire ministry. My family moved across town to live on the property which was owned by the ministry, and that was home for me until I entered college and eventually married. Watching my parents choose God's will over a comfortable salary with great benefits set into motion a foundation and principle that has guided me all of my life.

Growing up, I loved being outdoors. I was the typical tomboy who loved riding go-carts, dirt bikes, and water skiing. Anything my brother could do I was challenged to do just as well even though he was four years my senior. I also enjoyed the domestic side of life; cooking and cleaning for my mom as she worked full-time outside of the home. At sixteen, part of the responsibilities in helping my mom was to take the weekly budgeted amount of money and purchase the groceries for the family. I always loved the challenge of buying everything mom needed for the week and coming home with change. Little did I know that learning to be frugal and being able to stretch a dollar would serve me well in the ministry that my husband and I would be called too.

Through my high school years I enjoyed accounting and anticipated pursuing a career in bookkeeping like my mother. This was fulfilled the last semester of my senior year of high school as I worked in the bookkeeping department of a local bank which enabled me to earn the money to follow the plans I had for my life. As I began to fulfill those plans, I took the next step and enrolled in classes at the community college as the tuition would be reimbursed by my employer. Little did I know that in a few months God would interrupt **my** agenda and call me to Bible College some 1,500 miles from home. Two weeks before the fall semester began I was on my way to Texas. His word says, "Many are the plans in a person's heart, but it is the Lord's purpose that prevails" (Proverbs 19:21). This would be the beginning of a life of faith and following God's divine plan for my life.

Giving your life to Christ is not only about having your sins forgiven or living your life from your own perspective; it is surrendering it all to Him and allowing Him to lead and guide you every step of the way. His purpose is to see you become all He has destined you to be, but how many times do Christians choose the path of least resistance and alter everything that God is trying to accomplish in their lives?

We must know, without a doubt, that God has a plan for our lives. His plan is for our good. When we come to this realization, then we will face life from a whole new perspective. As a Christian we will face obstacles that He has ordained in order to reveal things to us that can be learned no other way. However, many individuals turn the obstacle against God and blame Him for the hardship they are facing instead of accepting it and allowing Him to lead them through it.

The goal should be to face the obstacle, learn the "life lesson" and move on. In my mind I have always looked at "obstacles" as a hurdle that a runner needs to successfully cross. As a runner begins, the height of the hurdle is low enough for him to successfully cross it, but as his skills develop the hurdle is raised to higher levels. I see this same scenario in our Christian walk. With each spiritual hurdle that we face and cross, God is seeking to build our confidence and faith to move us to greater levels of trust and confidence in Him. As we face new challenges or obstacles in life, God's desire is for us to cross that hurdle successfully so that we can learn and develop areas of our life that need to be changed and tempered by the Holy Spirit. If we resist His leading then I believe we will stay at this point in our Christian walk until we learn the lesson(s) that He is trying to teach us. Our submission to His will and leading is vitally important in our walk with God, as well as in our growing in God. We can make it difficult and painful if we continually resist His guidance. The choice is ours. Do we submit and follow His leading or resist and face the hurdle again? I cannot tell you that I have successfully submitted 100% of the time to His leading, but my motto has usually been "God, let me learn what you want me to learn, because I do not want to cross this hurdle again."

There have been many breaking points because many of the tests and hardships I have faced came unexpectedly; nor were they chosen or anticipated, but God has been with me every step of the way. As He led me through these times He showed Himself mighty and strong on my behalf as I was broken before Him.

That is the journey I would like you to travel with me....not to bring glory to myself, but to reveal God's faithfulness through every obstacle that has tried to obstruct my path and hinder my progress of growing in Christ. All of this has been orchestrated by God and designed to draw me closer to Him. He tells us in His word, "If you suffer as a Christian, do not be ashamed, but praise God that you bear that name" (1 Peter 4:16). I trust that as you read about the hardships and struggles that I have faced, you will know that God is there for you as well, and will sustain you through everything that comes your way if you yield and submit yourself at His feet.

Along this journey of serving Christ there will be spiritual warfare where you combat the enemy of your soul. However, God has reminded us in 1Timothy 6:12 that we are to "fight the good fight of faith." There will also be circumstances and situations that desire to rob you of your peace. However, the word of God reminds us in Philippians 4:7 to allow "the peace of God....to guard your hearts and your minds."

As mothers we desire to nurture our children and protect them from any harm, but in order to prepare them for the real world there comes a point where we have to allow them to learn to spread their wings and take flight. That is why I always thought it was best for my children to learn life lessons through experience. So it is in our walk with God. Experience teaches that the best lessons in life are learned when we face obstacles and sometimes even experience failure. God sees the potential in these times to teach us something we need to learn. God may even allow us to experience seasons of humility before He chooses to bring advancement and promotion. In this humbling process He reminds us that His strength is made perfect in our weakness (2 Corinthians 12:9). As we humble ourselves and yield to His leading

He proves again that His grace is sufficient to see us through.

As a child of God, we will face obstacles. The word **"obstacle"** means, **"something that obstructs or hinders progress."**[i] In the Old Testament we see Job's life as an example of a man who followed after God. Remember, Satan appeared before God and had to seek permission to test Job. Although he was severely tested, he made it through the test, yet it cost him his family and his possessions. In the middle of it all he expresses that his plans and the desires of his heart are shattered (see Job 17:11). Job 23:10-11 says, "But he knows the way that I take; when he has tested me, I will come forth as gold. My feet have closely followed his steps; I have kept to his way without turning aside." What an awesome conclusion of a man who lost everything, yet he remained true to God in the good and bad times. As a result of passing the test, God eventually restored, many times over, everything that had been taken from him.

Job's life exemplifies God's faithfulness when life is wonderful or overwhelming. Maybe God is bragging on you just as he bragged on Job, because He knows you will remain faithful to Him even when the bottom falls out of your world. If you have never thought about trials and obstacles from that perspective, then I admonish you to prayerfully look at it from this point of view. Instead of resisting what God may be trying to do in your life and just focusing on the situation, set your gaze above it, and ask God what He wants you to learn through this time of testing.

~ 2 ~

Learning Independence

"Have I not commanded you?
Be strong and courageous. Do not be afraid;
do not be discouraged, for the Lord your God
will be with you wherever you go."
Joshua 1:9

*A*s I mentioned in the last chapter, **my** life plans and agenda were set in place at seventeen years of age. While enrolled in the community college with what looked like a great career path set for me, God suddenly got my attention. The Bible College where my brother and sister were attending had an evangelistic team that traveled during the summer months. One Sunday night in August of 1978, the team ministered at my home church and through that

25

service God spoke to my heart. As a result of God getting my attention during that service, I knew that He wanted more from me; therefore, I **went to the altar and told God "yes" to whatever plans He had for my life.** That meant leaving behind a boyfriend, a full-time job, and all of my college courses which had been paid for by my employer. Within two weeks I sent my application to the college, packed up my car, and traveled 1,500 miles from home to answer the call of God on my life. I had $1,000 in my savings account and had no idea how far that would take me, but I began this adventure of a life of faith and obedience to God.

Saying goodbye to everything I knew and loved was one of the hardest things I have ever done in my life. Following God's will and answering the call of God is never an easy task, but having His hand of blessing upon your life because you "obeyed His call" is worth it all. The steps of obedience were forcing me and teaching me how to be strong and learn to stand on my own two feet. As a freshman in college I had to learn to step out of my comfort zone, find employment, and face life with all that it had to offer.

Once I arrived in Texas I knew that I had to work to put myself through college; therefore, I immediately began to look for a job that would be complimentary to my college schedule. The first place I interviewed became my place of employment for the next two years that I attended college in Texas. I did not know it until after I was hired, but one of the key employees within this company knew our family well and had been a part of our church many years prior in Florida. When he saw my name on the application he told the owner, "If she is anything like her mother, then you definitely need to hire her." I was so appreciative that day for my mother's reputation and strong work ethic because this helped me get a job. I am still thankful today for her Godly example that she has lived before me through the years.

After two years of attending Bible College in Texas, God directed my path to transfer to another Bible College, in my home state of Florida, which was only four hours from home. To my surprise, **my act of obedience to God's leading** would cause a setback in my life. Transferring from one college to another at the time was discouraging and somewhat disappointing. This act of obedience caused me to lose one year of college credit.

As we travel down life's road, God will ask us to do things that do not make sense in the natural, but somehow He is working it all for our good. Jeremiah 29:11 says, "For I know the plans I have for you," declares the Lord, "plans to prosper you and not to harm you, plans to give you hope and a future." In obedience, I followed God's leading and that year met the man that I would later marry. The year I transferred to the college in Florida was my husband's senior year. Had I not been obedient to **God's timing**, our paths would not have crossed.

I completed four years of college before I was married, but still needed one year to complete my degree in Education due to the year I lost in the transfer. Getting married moved me away from the college that I was attending, so I began to search for a school that would accept my course work in Virginia where my husband and I were living. Through my search I began to hit a wall no matter where I turned. Finally, I found a college that would accept three of the four years that I had already completed. I finished my final and fifth year and received my degree in Elementary Education. I would have loved to graduate from the college in Florida, but they did not offer distance education at that time, and we lived 1,000 miles from the college. Therefore, the possibility of that dream ever being fulfilled was virtually impossible.

My husband and I did not have your typical courtship due to the 1,000 miles that separated us. Over the course of a year we wrote letters and made many phone calls (that was before cell phones, so the monthly rates were quite large). Through prayer and the peace of God leading our hearts, we knew that God had brought our lives together. We were married in his home church where he served as the Associate Pastor. Let me add here that just because we obey God's will and His leading for our lives does not mean the road will be easy. When I said "I do" at the ripe old age of twenty-one I instantly became a pastor's wife to 600 people that I did not know. I was raised in a very different culture than my husband and moving to a new location was quite an adjustment for me. Needless to say, this was a growing time in my life, and I would not trade it for anything because I learned many valuable things about being a pastor's wife and being in the ministry.

You may be thinking, you should have just stayed at the college and finished your last year. That makes sense in the natural, and conventional wisdom would mandate that, but rarely does God lead through man's way of thinking. Through much prayer and God's leading, we both knew this was the right time for our marriage.

~ 3 ~
Gone, but not Forgotten

"For you created my inmost being; you knit me together in my mother's womb. I praise you for I am fearfully and wonderfully made; your works are wonderful, I know that full well."
Psalm 139:13-14

After being married for eighteen months my husband and I decided it was time to start a family. It was in the fall of the year and Christmas would be a great time to reveal the coming of a grandchild to our parents and loved ones. Since there were no grandchildren at all on either side of the family, our plan was to reveal my pregnancy by writing a note in a beautifully wrapped box and placing it under the Christmas tree. When our parents opened the box, the note would be written in first person from our son or daughter introducing themselves to their grand-parents. About six weeks into the pregnancy our dreams where shattered.

The unraveling of our dream began on a cold December morning in Virginia. My husband and I had dressed for work and decided to go to a local restaurant and grab a biscuit. It was December 2nd and the dew had made a frozen glaze on the ground. As we walked from the car to the restaurant, I walked over the wheelchair ramp which was connected to the sidewalk and hit a slick spot. As a result, I fell face first on the sidewalk and hit my stomach very hard. I was scheduled to meet the doctor that morning, but my husband was unable to go with me to the doctor's appointment since we taught school together. When I arrived at the doctor's office, I was told that my pregnancy was confirmed pos-itive, but I was unable to see the doctor because he had to tend to an emergency at the hospital. I mentioned to the nurse in charge that I had recognized some abnormalities. He told me to stay off of my feet and come to the hospital if there were any problems.

As I returned to school to finish out the day my husband and I were elated about the confirmed pregnancy, and excited that we would soon become parents. I took the doctor's advice and tried to sit as much as possible that day, however I had already made plans to attend a Tupperware party that evening with a friend. As the evening progressed my abnormalities got worse and I left the party early. Upon my arrival at the house I told my husband that we better get to the hospital. Just that morning the pregnancy test was positive, but that night in the hospital, my world turned upside down and the pregnancy test was negative. I was literally shaking on the inside due to all of the news and uncertainty. This was also my first experience of being a patient in a hospital.

During those days there was no such thing as a private room so I shared a room with another patient. The hospital would not allow my husband to stay in the room with me so I spent that agonizing night alone. As the night hours went by I tried to follow the nurse's instructions to rest, but I was in excruciating pain. I called a nurse who administered a shot of medication and held my hand until I went off to sleep. That was one of those nights when I could not even pray for myself. I felt all alone in this world and my parents were 800 miles away and my husband had gone home to rest.

The next day procedures were done to confirm that I had lost the baby, so my doctor arranged for me to head to surgery for the standard procedure to complete the miscarriage. I was hurting emotionally from all that I had gone through. It had all happened so fast. At the beginning of the day I was on cloud nine excited about the newness of becoming a mother and at the close of the day that little life had been taken from me. Once again I came face-to-face with the uncertainty of life.

My doctor was wonderful and comforting through the whole situation. His words helped me get through the difficult time and his assurances gave me hope that one day I would have a normal pregnancy and deliver a healthy baby. However, I still had questions. I also experienced a certain amount of sorrow and grieving that comes with any loss and death.

Right after the miscarriage I had to attend a baby shower for a lady in the church who was having her third child. It was one of those times that I did not want to go, but I attended out of obligation due to my role as a pastor's wife. I remember sitting there and saying, "God, this is not fair. I do not even have a child and she is on number three. Why do I have to sit here and act like I am happy for her? I am hurting, God. The pain is too fresh. I just want to get up, run away, and cry my eyes out."

Many times in life we go through situations and we think that we will never see our hopes materialize nor have the desires of our hearts fulfilled. There are times when there seems to be no joy in serving God; we feel like we do it more out of obligation than love. Somehow our devotion and commitment to Christ pull us along in those difficult times. God loves us more than we can ever imagine and He has a plan that is unique for us. In our discouragement and disappointment we can get our eyes on others and wonder why they are being blessed and have all the things that we desire. During those times we have to obey God's word and pray that they are blessed even though we are empty-handed and broken-hearted.

Every year on the third of December my mind goes back to that day when I lost our first child. At times I think about the day when I will be reunited with a son or daughter who has gone on before me. Time has not healed the pain, but God has.

When I lost the child, my parents sent money to purchase a Christmas arrangement in memory of the baby. Even though the arrangement has been mangled through the years due to storing it, our family knows what it represents. Several years ago I was going to throw it away, but my grown children said, "Mom, you can't." It represents a child that we never had the opportunity to hold or experience life with, but we know that one day we will be reunited with our son or daughter for eternity. That is the hope we hold on to.

I know that if I am this touched by a pregnancy that was just getting started and ended in a miscarriage, how much more do women suffer in silence when they have chosen to terminate a pregnancy somewhere in their past. The memory and pain seem to torment and it rarely ever goes away. Let me remind you that there is an all-loving God who is there to comfort and forgive you no matter what you have experienced or done in life. Will the memory of that child ever go away? Probably not, but God's grace and love are sufficient to heal the hurt that many women feel and struggle with. If that is you, then I ask you to totally give it to God. Allow Him to heal you as only He can do. God can take the pain of the past and turn it into a message for His glory and honor.

~ 4 ~

Unforeseen Obstacles

"I waited patiently for the LORD;
he turned to me and heard my cry.
He lifted me out of the slimy pit, out
of the mud and mire; he set my feet on a rock
and gave me a firm place to stand."

Psalm 40:1-2

*I*n a day and age of technological advances it is hard to believe that pregnancies can end abruptly. There is so much excitement and expectation that goes along with the wonder and awe of expecting a child. After the miscarriage my doctor suggested that I wait a few months before trying to get pregnant again. Nine weeks later, God was gracious and I was pregnant for the second time. Little did I know that my doctor was keeping a close eye on me during those first few months of my second pregnancy. While attending my fifth month check-up, the doctor looked at me and said, "I believe we have a baby." I did not realize how critical the situation had been, but my doctor never let on that he was concerned. The delivery was normal, but as I reflect on the few months after our son's birth, I probably experienced some postpartum depression as well, but I just chalked it up to a lack of sleep as he woke up every two hours around the clock desiring to be fed.

My third pregnancy was emotionally difficult due to a chemical or hormonal imbalance within my body. I experienced mood swings, depression, and some anxiety. My husband and I thought that it would pass once I gave birth, but it only intensified. Trying to be strong for everyone else, I hid the depression from our congregation and relatives. No one knew what I was experiencing except God and my husband. As a result, it began to take its toil on our marriage. At one point my husband was ready to quit the ministry, because he could not handle the stress of my situation and the demands of the pastorate. Knowing the call that God had placed upon his life just magnified the stress level in my own life as I felt responsible for the added stress that my depression was causing him.

On the flipside of it all, I knew that God had healed me many times throughout my life, so I knew He was able to take care of this situation as well. However, six years later I still struggled with depression and literally prayed everyday to die. The pain was so great that I thought dying was my only way out. I literally asked God to allow some tragedy to take place so that the pain and misery would end and my husband could find a new wife and my children could have a new mom. Imagine the emotional pain and turmoil of being the pastor's wife and hiding this from your church family and relatives, only to release the emotional pain on your husband and children. I knew this was the only safe place to let it out, so they bore the brunt of my emotional sickness and instability.

Before this battle with depression I was always a stable person who enjoyed life. If someone told me that they were dealing with depression I would say to myself, "Nothing can be that bad, just pick yourself up and get over it." I had been judgmental of others thinking that this was something they could control. Now, for the first time in my life, all of this was being brought into question as I was experiencing it all first hand.

Sickness, setbacks, and difficulties can come upon us dramatically and unexpectedly. These situations can strike without warning and leave us in a crisis characterized by anger, denial, withdrawal, and fear. Every circumstance is different, but we should not be ashamed or embarrassed to ask for or seek help.

I must say that my strong Christian heritage was the main thing that kept me during this difficult time. I finally received medical help and the doctor put me on anti-depressant medication. Through all of this I never lost sight of the fact that God could heal me. One day in the spring of the year, after being on medication for about three years, God made it clear to me that I was healed. I contacted my doctor of how to come off of the medication safely. She guided me and I walked in faith and obedience to receive my healing. If I had looked at the circumstances I may not be healed today. After God told me I was healed, I suffered two rough months emotionally. I had a choice; to look at the physical evidence or stand upon God's word. I stood on God's word that says, "He himself bore our sins in his body on the cross, so that we might die to sins and live for righteousness; by his wounds you **have been** healed" (1 Peter 2:24).

Through the years I have questioned why I had to go through this painful experience. The only definite answer that I see through God's word is that the sufferings we face help to strengthen others who will face the same challenges in life. Second Corinthians 1:3-5 tells us, "Praise be to the God and Father of our Lord Jesus Christ, the Father of compassion and the God of all comfort, who comforts us in all our troubles, **so that we can comfort those in any trouble with the comfort we ourselves have received from God**. For just as we share abundantly in the sufferings of Christ, so, also, our comfort abounds through Christ." God has truly given me countless opportunities to help others who are dealing with issues of depression. At the time of my suffering I did not understand the "why" of it all. Through hindsight I can see how God used it to bring glory to His name. Psalm 40:1-3 is truly a proclamation of my life having walked through the depths of depression. The psalmist David writes, "I waited patiently for the Lord; he turned to me and heard my cry. He lifted me out of the slimy pit, out of the mud and mire; he set my feet on a rock and gave me a firm place to stand. He put a new song in my mouth, a hymn of praise to our God. Many will see and fear and put their trust in the Lord." I only pray that this will be true of my life just as it was for David in the Old Testament; for we serve a God who is the same yesterday, today, and forever.

Setbacks

"For I know the plans I have for you," declares the Lord, "plans to prosper you and not to harm you, plans to give you hope and a future."
Jeremiah 29:11

*L*ife was beginning to move along at a fast pace as our kids were now school age and I was heavily involved in assisting and leading many ministries within the church. Through the busyness, I had managed to finish my fifth year of college and receive my bachelor's degree in Elementary Education. I spent several years working as a preschool teacher, and at this time, I was teaching second grade at a small Christian school in Virginia.

Things were going smoothly until I was told that I needed to acquire a certain certification to continue teaching. Upon sending in my transcripts and required information I was notified that I would have to go back and pick up necessary coursework to continue teaching due to some certification issues. How in the world could this be? I already had five years of college credits just to obtain a four-year degree.

I knew God's calling on my life was to Christian Education. As a general rule, Christian schools usually struggle financially due to the fact that they are totally tuition driven. Therefore, my pay as an Elementary Christian educator was low with no benefits. That was never an issue with me as long as I was in God's will. However, I remember thinking how could I afford to go back to school on such a small income already? Ultimately, I knew that God was my source and He had always met my needs so there was no reason to doubt His provision in my life now.

One night I was so distraught with all of this and through my tears I said to God, "What's the use? Why does it have to be so hard?" He gently spoke these words to my heart, "You don't see the whole thing." Even though the challenge was still ahead of me, I held on to those words that God had spoken so clear to my heart. I also made a comment to my husband during this season of my life, **"Maybe one day God will let me have a job in the area of teacher certification so that others will not have to go through what I have experienced."** You better be careful what you ask for because God may give you the desires of your heart and you just might get it all.

I began to pursue colleges that would work with me and this process was like walking down a dead-end street and hitting a brick wall. No matter which direction I turned, I received letter after letter of rejection from colleges and institutions that were unable to help me. Talk about questioning God. At this point I thought it would be better to just throw in the towel and do something else.

As a last resort I contacted the college I attended in Florida (the college I always wanted to graduate from) and to this day I will never forget the words from the registrar's mouth. As we spoke on the phone his words still ring clear in my mind as he said, "I know exactly what you need. You can pick up nineteen hours through the distance education program and receive a second Bachelor's degree to satisfy your certification requirements." Well, how do you like that? No one but God knew that I had always desired to graduate from this college, but, if you recall, I followed God's leading and got married instead of finishing my last year of studies at that university.

Once I enrolled in the distance education program I was informed that the program would be shutting down in about eighteen months. Talk about pressure; here I was teaching school full-time, being a mom to two children, a full-time pastor's wife and trying to complete course work within a shortened timeline. What other choice did I have? This was the only accredited school that was going to be able to help me, and if I did not have everything completed before the program closed down then I would lose everything I had ever worked for as far as my education was concerned. Needless to say, I laid out a timeline and got busy.

I completed everything on time and graduated with my second Bachelor's degree in the spring of 1998. Earning this degree also fulfilled a desire of my heart. The desire was delayed by sixteen years, but it was eventually fulfilled. Remember delay is not denial. If God spoke it, He will do it; if He promised you something, He will bring it to pass....not in your timing, but His. There is one stipulation; you have to be willing to follow His plan for your life.

Many times in life we follow God's leading and it does not make any sense. At those times we must remember that His timing is not synchronized with ours. Since His plan is much greater than ours, time is not a limitation to Him. In many circumstances in my life, hind sight has revealed that He was working on the other end to coordinate a situation designed specifically for my life. In other cases I still do not have all the answers; I've just had to learn to trust His leading. Some things I may not know until eternity and then I guess it really will not matter anyway.

Many Christians bail out too soon. They look at the circumstances of life and think that God has forgotten about them. Instead of trusting God for the outcome, they take matters into their own hands and try to help God out. This lack of trust ultimately delays what God is trying to teach us in life and many times we just make a mess out of it all. Ultimately, we may hinder God's plan for our lives and alter everything that He is orchestrating for our good and His glory.

In my mind I liken life to a marathon. It is all about persistence, hard work and endurance. If you talk to life-long runners, they will tell you that one principle remains constant and that is their devotion to putting in the miles. Therefore my motto has always been, "Learn what you need to the first time so you don't have to cross this hurdle again." How much more should we be committed as followers of Christ to press on with that same determination in mind? Paul penned it well when he said, "I press on toward the goal to win the prize for which God has called me heavenward in Christ Jesus" (Philippians 3:14).

~ 6 ~

Trusting in the Dark

"In my distress I called to the Lord; I cried to my God for help. From his temple he heard my voice; my cry came before him, into his ears."
Psalm 18:6

*N*ow that I had picked up nineteen more college credits and earned my second Bachelor's degree in Christian Education, I provided my transcripts so that I might obtain the certification that my employer required. As I waited to hear from the accreditation association, I am sure that my hopes waivered and my thoughts were not very positive due to all of the setbacks that I had already experienced. I will never forget the day that the response came in the mail. As I opened the large envelope, I think

I prepared myself for the worst. Much to my surprise, at the bottom of the page it said "Life-Time Bible Waiver." The year of Bible College, that I thought was a wash many years before was actually accepted and recognized. I thought a year of my education was wasted, but God knew the outcome the whole time. I just had to wait twenty-three years for the answer and I still have the paperwork filed away in a folder as a reminder of God's faithfulness.

Let me add here that a year of studying God's word is never wasted, but in the context of trying to earn my degree I felt as if I had spun my wheels for a year and no one recognized it. I did all of this in obedience to God's leading and direction for my life. The "Life-Time Bible Waiver" that was granted will continually satisfy my Bible credits for as long as I hold a teaching certification with this association. Having the waiver meant I did not have to take a Bible course every five years due to the amount of Bible that was taken while attending the first college that God directed me to. If God has given you a promise, He will be faithful to fulfill it (Ezekiel 24:14, KJV).

Maybe you have been trusting God for a certain situation in your life and it has not come to pass. Maybe you have experienced things that do not make sense. Let me encourage you to trust God to work it out. I know that there are still things I do not understand within my own life, but my responsibility is to trust God and live in obedience to Him and His word. Many times I just hold on to the promise that says, "And we know that all things work together for good to them that love God, to those who are the called according to his purpose" (Romans 8:28).

As I continued to walk in obedience to God's leading and teach in Christian schools, I would often question God as to why I had to earn a second Bachelor's degree. I had been obedient in following His leading, so why did it all have to be so difficult? At that time I did not realize that I would need the second Bachelor's degree to open doors that God would ask me to walk through years later. As time progressed I applied for state certification and needed transcripts from both colleges. I sent certified letters to the college where I obtained my first degree, but they continued to be returned since they were no longer in existence. My husband was teaching as an adjunct professor at the college where I obtained my second degree, so he went to the registrar's office to see about obtaining copies of my transcripts. Now, you can label what I am about to share with you as a coincidence, but I choose to see it as God's divine intervention in my life. The day my husband entered the registrar's office to obtain an official copy of my transcripts was the week that this college was cleaning out old records, condensing files, and archiving older files. It had been twenty-three years since I had first enrolled in this college, so condensing files would be a necessary task for any institution as it continued to grow.

You see, this college was the only institution who had an official copy of my transcript from where I earned my first Bachelor's degree. As a result, they were able to send an official copy of my transcript to the Department of Education of the state where I was currently teaching. This satisfied all of the requirements for the state and I was able to obtain my teaching certificate. Once again, God showed me that He had everything in control, and He was proving to me that He was faithful to bring it to pass.

Three years after I acquired my state teaching certificate, the door of opportunity opened for me to go back to school and obtain my Master's degree. I filled out the application and sent the required documents. Thinking that all was well, I contacted the University to inquire when I could begin the graduate program. They informed me that they still needed the transcript from the college where I earned my first degree. I told them that the school was no longer in existence and asked them what I should do. They informed me that I needed to contact the Board of Regents, in that state and they needed to document that the college I attended was accredited and open during the date that I graduated. I followed their instructions and spoke with the Administrative Assistant to the president of the Board of Regents. What are the chances of having an individual in the right place to confirm what I needed? As I spoke with the Administrative Assistant, she distinctly remembered the college and said that she would take care of it for me. She took my need before the president of the Board of Regents and he supplied the documentation that was needed for me to be accepted at the university so that I could begin my Master's program.

What impossible challenge are you facing today? Are you trying to solve it in your own strength? Well, let me encourage you today to be persistent. Don't give up too soon. If you do, you just might rob yourself of the biggest blessings that God desires to give you. He has a plan and answer to everything that you face, and it is so much greater than you can ever imagine.

How many times do we question God when we hit a wall instead of trusting Him? When we give our life to Christ, do we really trust Him to work everything out? Trust comes through experience. The longer we walk with Christ and allow Him to lead, the more we can trust Him as He leads us through deeper and longer valleys.

Do not curse the dark! Once again the age old question is "Why do the righteous suffer?" Only God can truly answer that question. His promise is that He will be with us in all of life's ups and downs, trials and tribulations, joys and sorrows, and He will help us to be victorious through them all.

~ 7 ~

Tough Love

"Husbands, in the same way be considerate as you live with your wives, and treat them with respect as the weaker partner and as heirs with you of the gracious gift of life, so that nothing will hinder your prayers."

I Peter 3:7

s a little girl I loved to dress up in my mom's dresses, put on her gloves, carry one of her big purses, and clomp through the house in her high heels. Feeling all grown up, I would play house and push my baby dolls around in the stroller nurturing and caring for them just like my mom. All of this imaginary play was mirroring an inner desire to one day grow up, find my "prince charming," and live happily ever after. That day finally came at the age of twenty-one. I grew up, said "I do," and, after a few years, reality set in. You see, there is nothing about a marriage, a mortgage, a mother-in-law, or a parsonage in the mountains that guarantees happiness, yet this is what most of us desire.

I think many of us enter marriage thinking it is all going to be wonderful and bliss...problem free. I know that when I got married, I thought my husband would make everything complete and fill every void in my life. When that did not happen, then I was hurt and disappointed. It has taken years for me to realize that I had probably placed very unrealistic expectations upon him. To expect one person to do all and be all is a very tall order for anyone to fill under the best of circumstances.

Any marriage will have its challenges, but adding the role and responsibilities of pastoring on top of that can be very overwhelming at times. We all have areas of our lives that are better than others, and some areas take a little more effort. For the first five years of our marriage everything was going great! My husband and I had obeyed God's leading for our lives in marrying each other, and things in the ministry were progressing very nicely for us. However, around the seven year mark our relationship was being put to the test.

For the first five years of our marriage my husband served as an associate pastor. As we continued to follow God's direction for our lives, we felt it was time to step out and my husband was voted in as Senior Pastor of our first church. As we looked forward to this new journey and chapter in life, we discussed the areas of our life and ministry that we thought would be difficult, versus the areas that we thought would be easy. The one area that my husband and I felt secure in was our relationship with each other. We were pastoring our first church and enjoying parenting our young son. I was continuing my education while my husband was working on his first Master's degree and life was just demanding and busy. Since the church was small and the pay was minimal, I agreed to work full-time so that my husband could devote all of his time to the church.

Since this was the first church we had ever pastored, we were very excited about the possibilities before us. God gave us favor with the congregation as we earned their respect and began to see great things take place. Many doors of opportunity were opening for my husband to minister on the local and international level. On the local level, the congregation was growing numerically and spiritually which enabled us to improve the property and facilities, as well as add more ministries. My husband was also on a weekly TV broadcast which was seen throughout the state. Internationally, God opened the door for my husband to minister on a radio program in West Africa. Each week, through this broadcast, my husband had the potential of reaching 300 million English speaking Africans with the gospel of Jesus Christ. We began to receive correspondence assuring us that many people were coming to Christ as a result of this ministry. One letter I specifically recall was from several former witch doctors who had surrendered their lives to Jesus Christ as a result of hearing the broadcast. Wow, we were excited!

Anytime God begins to bless, the devil begins to mess. We have seen this over and over again in our ministry. Many people were coming to know Christ as their Lord and Savior through the efforts of our ministry, and the enemy was not going to take this lying down. We had a target on our backs and his arrows were hot. My husband and I began to argue all the time which was not common for our marriage. Several months into these arguments, I looked at my husband and said, "Don't you recognize the problem?" He responded by saying, "Yes, the problem is you." Isn't that how we usually look at problems? Surely it cannot be us who has the problem, but the other person.

From the beginning of creation we have been passing the buck; pointing the finger to the other person for things that seemingly go wrong in our lives. When things do not measure up, we miss the mark and feel that we have done all we can do, then we "shift the blame." All we have to do is go back to the beginning of Genesis and see the first example of this with Adam and Eve in the Garden of Eden.

When my husband passed the blame on to me, I responded by saying, "No, this is spiritual warfare." Anytime we mess in Satan's territory, he is going to do everything he can to try and defeat us. Once my husband and I recognized where the friction was coming from, we were able to pray accordingly and defeat the enemy of our souls.

I am not saying that all marital problems are ultimately caused by spiritual warfare. Sometimes it is just our selfish nature and stubbornness. Sometimes we just want to be right or have our own way so we sacrifice the relationship at the expense of our spouse's feelings and needs. I would like to tell you that my husband and I have never had any other problems in our thirty years of marriage, but that would not be true. However, we are committed to working at our marriage on a daily basis. Many times I think of the words that were spoken to us at our wedding by Rev. Max Linkous, "What God hath brought together, let no man put asunder."

Within the marital relationship, problems can usually be categorized into three areas: financial, communication, and sexual. If you are married, hopefully, you are not experiencing problems with any or all of these areas. If your marriage is problem free and blissful, then I would like to meet you. In almost thirty years of ministry I have only met one couple that said they never had any problems. In my opinion, one of the partners was doing all the giving and one doing all the taking. Any relationship in life takes effort and work. Love is truly a commitment and not a feeling, because sometimes the feelings are there and sometimes they are not. A Christian marriage must have Christ at the center and must strive to keep Him as the central focus of the marriage's source and strength.

A major issue in some marriages is the lack of communication, as well as miscommunication. When these issues are not resolved, it can lead to problems with conflict management. "Many people think it is the 'big' things in a relationship that cause divorce like infidelity and abuse. However, most marriages end because of uncommunicated differences and unresolved conflicts about everyday things."[ii] When couples do not deal with unresolved conflict, it is like rust that slowly erodes and weakens a piece of steel. Steve Wickstrom, a free-lance writer, in his article *Resolving Conflict in Your Marriage* puts it this way, "Rust is a product of nature. Conflict is a product of human nature. In any marriage conflict is inevitable. It is not a matter of if conflict will arise, but when it will happen. Unresolved conflict is the rust of marriage." It leads to "unforgiveness, emotional wounds, hurt feelings, bitterness, and possibly divorce."[iii] If you struggle in this area, I encourage you to seek help, make every effort to learn how to deal with conflict so that it does not eat away at your marriage relationship.

There is a reason that God instructs us to not let the sun go down on our wrath. That is because when issues are not resolved, it puts distance between you and your spouse. It also hinders the relationship with God because we see Peter's command when he says, "Husbands, in the same way be considerate as you live with your wives, and treat them with respect as the weaker partner and as heirs with you of the gracious gift of life, so that **nothing will hinder your prayers**" (1 Peter 3:7). Therefore, you should always work to keep the lines of communication open, respect each other, and seek the greatest good for one another.

Marriage by God's design is meant to be a picture of Christ and the church; a relationship like none other on earth. A covenant made with God between a husband and a wife; it is not a contract to be easily broken. When we give our lives to Christ our natural response should be to love and serve Him freely; not out of obligation or duty. The scriptures clearly instruct husbands to "love your wives, just as Christ loved the church and gave himself up for her" (Ephesians 5:25). Paul went on to say, "Husbands ought to love their wives as their own bodies. He who loves his wife loves himself. After all, no one ever hated his own body, but they feed and care for their body, just as Christ does the church" (Ephesians 5:28-29). Nowhere in scripture does God instruct the wife to love the husband. If the husband truly loves his wife and gives of himself for her; meeting her needs, then her natural response is to love him back and freely give of herself to him. Her needs go way beyond the natural. Some men think that because they are a good provider that this is sufficient, but that is only meeting the needs of the "body." God created us body, soul, and spirit so there are needs within the other two areas as well.

In many marriages there is no natural flow of love and sacrificial giving. Instead it is self-centered and self-seeking; a relationship filled with dissention, friction, and unrest. Instead of seeking help and working on the situation, many couples divorce and move on. In some cases many couples stay together for the sake of the children and/or because they feel trapped and remain unhappy during the course of their marriage.

"According to The Enrichment Journal the divorce rates in America for first marriage is 41%; the divorce rate in America for second marriage is 60%; the divorce rate in America for third marriage is 73%. According to discovery channel, couples with children have a slightly lower rate of divorce than childless couples."[iv] Many studies show that the divorce rate is almost identical for Christians and non-Christians. That is a sobering thought. From this perspective it would seem that Christian marriages have no more hope than those who are non-believers. Could it be that marriages are falling apart because we are not following God's design?

Scriptures admonish husbands to love their wives. Proverbs 30:21-23 says, "Under three things the earth trembles, under four it cannot bear up; a servant who becomes king, a fool who is full of food, **an unloved woman who is married**, and a maidservant who displaces her mistress." Once again from scripture, we have a great reminder for husbands to love their wives. King Solomon in all of his findings in life found this to be true. He must have known because he had 700 wives and 300 concubines. Proverbs 19:13 says, "A quarrelsome wife is like a constant dripping." Similar verses continue with the same theme: Proverbs 21:9, "Better to live on the corner of a roof than share a house with a quarrelsome wife," Proverbs 21:19, "Better to live in a desert than with a quarrelsome and nagging wife," and Proverbs 27:15, "A quarrelsome wife is like the dripping of a leaky roof in a rainstorm." Ladies, I can tell you from experience that more is accomplished when you allow God to change your husband than your trying to make it happen in your own strength. The scriptures clearly spell out what nagging is to your husband. Need I say more? My suggestion is to hold your peace and hit your knees. God is the only one who can truly make the lasting change in your husband's life, and He can do it so much better than you ever dreamed possible.

Guys, I am not putting all of the responsibility upon your shoulders for the way your wife acts or the mood that she may be in. However, in most cases, one plays off of the other. It is not my desire within the scope of this book or chapter to address all the ins-and-outs of the marriage relationship, but if the husband will obey Scripture and love his wife unconditionally and sacrificially, then in most cases she will naturally love him back. His needs will be met and so will hers.

Why did God choose to use marriage as a picture of Himself and the Church? Could it be there is more to marriage than we ever dreamed? We know that God is the author and designer of love and He demonstrated sacrificial love by sending His Son to die on the cross for our sins in order that we might be redeemed back to Him. So, what better way could there be for us to see symbolism than the marriage between a man and woman. Never in the history of time and the church have we ever seen this institution under such an attack as we do today.

Gals, we are to honor and respect our husbands. It is your responsibility to pray for him, encourage him, affirm him, and be his biggest fan. Believe in his dreams, and then back them up when he pursues them. If your husband grew up hearing the words "you will never amount to anything," then that is what he brings into the marriage. It may take him a lifetime to overcome that, but you are the most powerful influence in helping him overcome that hurdle in his life. Remember, there is life and death in the power of the tongue (Proverbs 18:21).

It is hard to believe that my husband and I will celebrate thirty years of marriage this year. When someone asks my husband how long we have been married he will respond, "Thirty years in a row....to the same woman!" Now-a-days that is quite an accomplishment. It has taken me and my husband thirty years to try and figure things out and we are still working at it. The key thing is staying committed, seeking help as needed and continually seeking God's favor and direction which we do on a daily basis. I wish I could tell you that we have always done the things I have listed, at all times, but we have not. However, we have never used the "D" word (divorce) with each other, even in the worst of times. We made this promise to each other before we got married and, by the grace of God, we have stuck to it. Within the appendix there are some recommended readings that I have found to be most helpful regarding marriage. (See Appendix A)

It should come as no surprise that this chapter is the longest one in the book. That is because amongst all of the obstacles I have faced, I have walked them out with my husband by my side. Have we always been on the same page with everything and every decision? No. However, through it all, our love has been "tough." True love is definitely a commitment and a choice; more giving than receiving.

As I wrap up this chapter, let me say a few words from the perspective of being a pastor's wife. There will be many demands that the congregation will try to put on you. It is okay to say "no." It took me thirty-five years of living to realize that I was allowed to let that word cross my lips. It is still hard for me to tell others no as I am very committed to the ministry and yet work at least forty hours outside of the home. However, it is important that wives do not sacrifice the needs of their husbands, children, and home at the expense of building the church. The proper sequence is God, your husband, your children, then the ministry. On the other hand, it is important to support the ministry in every way possible, but balance and boundaries are a must. Many times your husband's success as a pastor hinges on your faithful support. But when it is all said and done and the kids move on, it is just going to be you and your husband that is left. In all of your getting and doing within this journey of life, do not forget who you committed your life to......your spouse. When it is all said and done, I hope my husband can say that I was a true example of a Proverbs 31 woman.

~ 8 ~

Parenting PK's

"These commandments that I give you today are to be on your hearts. Impress them on your children. Talk about them when you sit at home and when you walk along the road, when you lie down and when you get up."

Deuteronomy 6:6-7

Parenting is one of the hardest jobs you will ever undertake, but it can be one of the most rewarding. I heard my husband say the other day that your children are the only thing on this earth that you can take to heaven. That is true; however, it is our responsibility as parents to do everything we can to bring them to the point of accepting Christ as their personal Savior at the age of accountability. It is up to them whether they accept Him to be the Lord and Savior of their lives.

God's word tells us that children are a heritage from the Lord, and we are blessed if we have them (Psalm 127:3-5). As parents, we have a responsibility to bring forth "Godly offspring" (Malachi 2:15); therefore, this is a privilege that cannot be taken lightly. I have often heard my husband tell the story of a lady who questioned Billy Graham as to when she should begin taking her little girl to church. He asked her how old her daughter was and she replied, "Seven." He told her, "My goodness woman, get her in church now, you are seven years behind."

If you are reading this and you did not become a Christian until later in your adult life, after your children were raised, you might be saying, "Great, here's another area where I have failed." Please do not look at it that way. God holds us accountable for what we know, not for what we do not know. On the other hand, if your children turned out great, praise God that you were able to have a part in seeing that happen. You may have children that you raised to love and serve God, they were in church every time the doors were open, and you saw to it that they studied the Word of God, but they are not presently serving the Lord. If that is the case, do not beat yourself up. Continue to pray for them and believe that God will restore them to where they need to be. When they are little, they step on our toes. When they are grown, they can step on our hearts. The bottom line is, when we place our heads on the pillow each night, we have to know that we have done our best. Just remember when raising kids, love must be tough, but it also needs to be unconditional as well. Know that the best you gave was good enough.

Children will totally change your world. They are an investment of your time, money, and energy. Somehow, they wrap themselves around our hearts. Many of us would sacrifice all that we have to see that they have what they need. However, in this process of meeting their needs it is important that your children do not come between you and your spouse. Many parents can become so entwined in raising the children that they neglect the needs of their spouse. Just remember, eighteen years will come and go very quickly, and it will be the two of you again, so do not allow yourselves to become strangers along the way.

Make time for each other. Have a date night every week. There were times that we only had money to go and get a cup of coffee, but we still got away. We had a dear friend in the church who was like an uncle to our kids, and they loved being with him. He would come over after work and play with the kids while we got away for a few hours. My husband was also good to give me a night every week just to get out of the house for a few hours to clear my head and unwind. I am very thankful that he was sensitive to my needs during those years.

Everything in our life is surrounded by boundaries and limits. That is a principle parents must teach their children from a very early age. In raising our children, no matter where we went, our children learned that the rules and expectations were the same. If they crossed the line, then they knew ahead of time what the consequences would be. You might think that sounds like "boot camp." Quite the contrary; the consistency proved that we loved our children enough to not let them get away with the disobedience and disrespect that they might attempt to display from time-to-time.

Children will always test your boundaries and limits that you set. That is human nature. It is your responsibility to follow through with them. If a boundary is worth setting, then it is worth enforcing. If it is unreasonable, get rid of it. However, children should not be able to manipulate you with their behavior, set the tone of the home with their actions or usurp your god-given authority to get their way. Children are more secure when they know where the boundary lines are and when those lines are enforced.

When it comes to raising PK's (Preacher's Kids) be reasonable with them. They cannot help that their parent happens to be a preacher. Do not put unnecessary demands upon them. They already have enough pressure to contend with from their peers and the fact that their parent is the pastor of the church they attend. That alone carries a big weight and responsibility.

One of the best things you can do for your pastor and his family is to pray for them daily. There are pressures they face that you know nothing about. There are demands on their time and schedules that are like none other. All of the years that we have served in ministry, we never had the privilege of living close to our relatives. Therefore, our children never had the privilege of growing up around their grandparents, aunts, uncles, and cousins. Some of the churches we pastored were sensitive to this issue and compensated for this; others were not. Yes, we visited our families as often as we could, and they reciprocated the visits too, but there still was a void.

When our kids were young we never told them that they could not do certain activities because they were "preacher's kids." If there were certain activities that we felt were not wholesome and they should not participate in, we sat down with them and showed them from scripture why the activity was not healthy for a Christian. I will add that we tried to be consistently faithful to live what we preached on a daily basis. Did we fail as parents? Oh yes, and when we did, we tried to go to them and apologize when we royally messed up.

Children do not pop out of the womb with an instruction manual. Therefore, as the parent, we must daily seek God's face for wisdom, discernment, and guidance as to how we will raise each child that we are blessed with. God gives us His word to guide us as we guide them. Remember, no two children are alike, so the guidance and discipline that may work for one child may not work for the second, third, and fourth child. Be sensitive to this and ask God to direct you as to what is best for their personality and temperament.

As my husband and I sought God's wisdom in guiding our children, I believe He gave my husband this insight for helping our son understand a great concept when he was little. One day our son wanted to participate in an activity with the neighbor boys that we did not think was wholesome. So, my husband pulled out a mouse trap, baited it with a piece of cheese, and told our son to take the cheese since he loved cheese so much. As you can imagine, he looked at his father in bewilderment that he would ask him to do something so bizarre. "Dad" he said, "I'm not taking that cheese because the trap will hurt me." "Exactly son," my husband replied. He went on to tell him how the mouse gets caught in the trap because all he sees is the cheese. That day he adequately expressed to our son that there are things in life you will have to trust me on because I am your father. Right now with this particular activity that you want to participate in, all you see is the cheese, but, as your father, I see the trap. From that time on, all my husband would have to say is, "Son, I see the trap" and our son would reply, "I know dad, all I see is the cheese."

As parents we are slowly working ourselves out of a job. There is a lot of territory to cover in eighteen short years. We bond, bond, bond when they come out of the womb. Then we help them crawl, stand on their own two feet, walk, and run. Every step is a process, and each day is an opportunity to guide them with Godly principles as they learn about life and build their independence. With the purest of efforts it is not an easy task and can be quite daunting at times because every child is unique. That is why God's word says, "Train up a child in the way he should go" (Proverbs 22:6, KJV). Notice that the pronoun is singular here, not plural. Every child is different and you have to deal with each one individually. Notice I did not say compromise principles; but in discipline and instruction, you must realize that they are unique, and God has a specific plan and design for their lives. It is our job as parents to help them find and nurture their talents.

Another important aspect in parenting is teaching your children about finances. We always gave our children chores and responsibilities without allowance. This was just part of being a family. However, we taught them financial integrity and responsibility through other avenues. Anytime they received money, by earning it or as a gift, we taught them to give ten-percent of the total to the church, as this was the tithe that God requires as stated in Malachi. We also instructed them to try and save a percentage of their money for their "rainy day" fund or for something they were working toward purchasing in the future. These are life principles that do not just happen. They have to be taught when children are small and continue to reinforce them through their teen years. Now our children are adults and on their own, yet they continue to show integrity in their stewardship with money.

It is important as parents that we pray daily with our children and pray specific prayers over their lives. From the day my husband became a Christian on April 16, 1975, he began to pray daily for whom he would marry and for the children God may allow him to raise. From the time our children were little; we had daily devotions and prayed with them. This was a daily discipline that we practiced, and we encouraged them to start having their own devotions as young teenagers. Once again, this is a discipline that has to be taught and we must set an example before them. We cannot assume that it will just happen. We teach a lot by what we say, more by what we do, but most by what we are.

Another aspect in parenting that was of the utmost importance to me was sharing the dinner meal together. Even though our lives were very busy with my working outside the home and being a pastor's wife, therefore I always protected that time. My husband and I have always shared the household and parenting responsibilities, therefore whoever got home first would begin cooking, and we would sit at the dinner table and eat our evening meal together. The TV was not on and we did not answer the phone. We spent this time talking about our day and always tried to get our kids to open up and tell us what was going on in their world or what events were coming up that we needed to add to the calendar. As our children got older and moved from their teen years into adulthood, one of my fondest memories was making a pot of coffee and talking about scripture and the things of God. There were exceptions, but that was the practice we normally followed.

When the kids were school age we made every Friday evening "family night." My husband and I tried to never put anything on our calendars or accept any invitations on Fridays. That was our family time and we worked hard to protect it. We usually went to a drive-in restaurant and ordered hamburgers and fries, then went home and watched several family shows on TV and played games. I know my kids may remember it a little differently; however, that is my recollection of those special nights together and they can never be taken away. Those will always be times that are precious to me and I will treasure them all of my life.

I would like to share a few clichés that we used while raising our children. Hopefully, they will become part of what you do with those children who are still in your care.

"Rules without a relationship foster rebellion." From the time children are very small they have to learn boundaries which are ultimately for their security and safety. You and your spouse must agree upon the rules that your children are expected to obey as long as they live under your authority. As they grow you may loosen the reigns a bit in some areas, but never compromise the principles and standards that guide your rules. If you remain consistently consistent, then your children will understand that no matter where you are (e.g., mall, grocery store, church, relative's home) the rules remain the same. The consistency of your "yes" and "no" can ultimately build trust between you and your child if it is done in love. In most cases your child will grow to understand that you have their best interest at heart.

If you are inconsistent in your rules and discipline, this just leads to frustration for your children. Trust and respect is not something that just happens in a parenting relationship; it must be earned and built over time. That is why we always said, "Rules without a relationship foster rebellion." As our children grew into adolescence we allowed them to sit down and talk to us respectfully if they did not agree with a decision we made or felt that we were being unfair. This was not a way for them to change our minds on the decision, but we listened to their point of view. Sometimes we did change our minds after the discussions, but many times we did not. We told our son and daughter that as their parents we felt that this was the best decision for them and ultimately, one day we will stand before God and give an account for what we allowed them to do.

"What you allow in moderation children will indulge in excess." Your children are always watching you. If you live a double standard, they will call your hand on it. Moms, teach your daughters how to be godly young ladies. Set guidelines in their dress. They can dress stylish and still be modest. Take them to scripture and discuss how they are responsible for their appearance. If a girl dresses in such a way to cause a young man to lust after her, then she is just as guilty as the young man for lusting after her. You may think that is harsh, but many young ladies dress with this intent.

On the other hand, Dads, how are you living before your sons? Are you setting a godly example in speech and conduct? Are you teaching them how to love and respect their future wife by the way you treat their mother? It all really comes down to daily living a holy life before those that God has entrusted into our care.

"If it's yes today, it's yes tomorrow. If it's no today, it's no tomorrow." Make sure you remain consistent. When you are not, it is confusing to children. It troubles me when I see a parent reasoning with a young child. When children are small they need you to be firm, fair, and friendly with your boundaries and expectations. Do not stand there and argue with them. You are the parent; set the rules and abide by them. As your child gets older, then you can sit down and talk about things if they think they are unreasonable. We did this with our children as they moved into adolescence. However, you are the parent and, ultimately, what you say is and should be the final answer.

"We teach a lot by what we say, more by what we do, but most by what we are." I think this one really sums up everything in parenting. There is really no explanation necessary here.

Three years ago my husband and I entered the "Empty Nesters" club. Some moms have a hard time with this transition. I miss my children, but if I know they are fine then I am fine. There comes a time for them to move on and begin their families; this is a part of life. I believe it is important to cut the apron strings and allow your children to establish their own families, yet be there to support them when they need you and/or seek your advice.

Our daughter and her husband live in town. Our son and his wife live in California with their new born son. As a result, we will move into a new chapter of life; becoming grandparents. I have always said that your job as a parent is not over once your children leave home, but it just continues on a larger scale. There are more things to pray about and more family members to embrace and love as the years go by and as new members are added to the family. We gave them to God when they were infants, dedicating them to God as a sign that they belong to Him, but realizing it was our responsibility to raise them in the nurture and admonition of the Lord.

~ 9 ~

"Can you live on that?"

*"Now to him who is able to do immeasurably
more than all we ask or imagine, according to
his power that is at work within us."*

Ephesians 3:20

I stated at the beginning of the book that
one of the welcomed challenges for me,
at sixteen years of age, was going to the grocery
store to buy the weekly groceries for the family
and coming home with change. Being competi-
tive by nature, I just enjoyed being able to show
my mom that I could save more money than
she could and come home with just as many
groceries (if not more) than she had. Little did I
know that my love for finding a bargain would

be a great asset in the ministry that my husband and I would be called to.

Many wives and moms are absorbed with the "couponing craze" and I think it is great. Perhaps I was just thirty years ahead of my time because that is how my family lived before "couponing" became the "in" thing to do. I think we should always find ways to save where we can and be wise with what we have. In the Kingdom of God we call that being a "good steward" of what God has entrusted to us.

After my husband had served in the role of Associate Pastor for thirteen years, God called us to pastor our first church. There was a certain city in North Carolina that my husband felt called to. After contacting the district superintendent, we found out that there was a church available in that area. He contacted the head board member at the church and scheduled a service for us to candidate for the senior pastor position that weekend.

For some reason God has given my husband the ministry of taking small, struggling churches and putting them back together again. In most cases the building is in need of repair, the finances are all but gone, and the members are few. With the leading of the Holy Spirit and God's guidance and strength we have taken four churches that match this description over the past twenty-five years. Since my husband's desire is to see the churches move forward, I have always agreed to assist the ministry by working full-time, outside of the home.

Before we were married we discussed the schedule, expectations, and demands of ministry. My husband said, "If you help bring home the bacon, I'll help fry it." He has stayed true to his word all of the years that we have been married. Many times I come home and he has cooked dinner and cleaned the house due to a very busy schedule for both of us. On the flip side of that, I help wash and wax the cars and sneak in mowing if his schedule is overflowing, although my rows are not as straight as he would like them. If the wife is working outside of the home, then it is unfair for her to come home and put in another forty hours with the household duties and raising the children.

Every church that God has called us to pastor has had very little money left in the bank when my husband accepted the pastorate. Therefore, his salary started out very minimal in comparison to his years of experience and educational degrees earned. We have never based the salary or lack of it as a sign of whether we should take the church. God has always dealt with our hearts through prayer and fasting of where and when we are to make a pastoral change. Through the interview a board member has asked my husband if he can live on a minimal amount of money because there is only a hand full of people left in the church. In many instances my husband responds to the board member(s) by saying, "I understand you have a family of four, "*Can you live on that*?" Once they regain their composure, they respond by saying, "Well, no." He politely says, "Well, I guess you answered your own question."

The ministry is not about our gain, but ultimately contributing to the body of Christ and following God's will as He directs our steps. Yes, it takes finances to live and survive in this world, but God's word clearly states that if we "seek first His kingdom, and his righteousness...all these things will be given to you as well" (Matthew 6:33). As our family put God first and even put Him to the test, He has proven faithful time and time again. We have faithfully done our part by not living above our means and always striving to live debt free. I am sure I embarrassed my children many times by pulling out coupons at a restaurant or turning their attention to the special on the menu, only to see them do the same thing now that they are on their own and picking up the tab.

One particular time in our first church we had more month than we had income. We were living on a tight budget, not living above our means; however, we just came up short that month. We did not know how we were going to make the house payment at the end of the month. My husband and I prayed about it and told no one else. Later that month a couple in our church invited some families over for pizza Sunday night after church. They asked my husband and me to stick around and we did. The gentleman handed my husband a check to which my husband said "thank you" and put it in his pocket. When we were getting in the car my husband pulled the check out and looked at it. He thought it was $100, but as he looked a second time, it was $1000. My husband and I turned around to return to the house to thank the couple for their generosity. They invited us back in the house and began to tell us how they had sold a house in another state and God had dealt with each of them individually to give us an exact amount of money. When they spoke to each other about it, they both said that God had given them the amount of $1,000. That was the amount we needed to get through this financial hardship. God had truly come through for us.

On another occasion we needed a new roof on our house. We prayed and looked at all of our options. We did not feel a peace to pull a second mortgage to cover it nor did we feel it was wisdom to empty the savings account to cover it. Therefore, the two of us continued to pray about it. During this time my husband's vehicle was accumulating some hefty miles, so we were going to have to purchase another car for him sooner than we expected. One day as my husband pulled the mail from the mailbox, there was a letter from a dear friend of ours who lived about 1,000 miles away. As he opened the card, our friend had written that God had directed him to send us $10,000. My husband and I stood in the kitchen in awe of what God had done as tears ran down our cheeks. That evening, for the first time, we shared with our children how God had answered this prayer that they knew nothing about. I might add here that my husband and I always tried to shield our children from the situations that might add stress to their lives. Many preachers' kids can feel enough stress due to their parents being in leadership, so we tried to protect them where we could until they were older. God had not only answered our prayer and supplied the money to pay for a new roof, but He also supplied money for a nice down payment on a new car that my husband needed.

I could add many more stories on top of that, but I think you understand the point I am trying to make. God has been faithful to us and met our needs just as He has promised He will do for all of us. As we faithfully do our part, He will be faithful to His word every time.

Does God really care? Can He do exceedingly, abundantly, above anything that we ask of Him? You bet He can and then some because He is a mighty God!

I have only mentioned a few of the financial miracles that God has provided for our family. The point is God is faithful. If we look to the natural circumstances then we are not truly living by faith. If God asks us to do a particular task, job or ministry, then it is our responsibility to obey and His responsibility to come through for us. Put Him to the test and see if He will not do exceeding and abundantly above all that we are able to ask or think of Him.

When God says, "No"

*"Bring joy to your servant, Lord,
for I put my trust in you."*
Psalm 86:4

Many times in our lives God will place us in situations where we question His plan and purpose. We know that He has directed us to a certain relationship, job, church, or situation, but the daily journey seems so hard. When we pray and ask God to release us from the assignment, He may say "No!" We forget that God uses these times to perfect our faith, and He also uses these situations to prove what is in our hearts. Once again we must remind ourselves that God's ways are not our ways.

My husband and I had been married for sixteen years and were pastoring in his home state. During the third year at this church God began to stir our hearts about moving to a particular city in another state. We prayed and sought God's direction and He placed a certain city upon our hearts; however, He did not open the door for us to make a move for two more years. The day finally came and we were voted in and made preparations to move. During one of the last services at the church, a lady in our church handed me a note. As she had been praying on my behalf, God revealed to her that I would be going through some great hardships, but, through all of it, God desired me to have joy. I thanked her and placed it in my Bible and said, "God, if this is really from You then it will come to pass."

We made the move and God opened the door for me to teach in a brand new school. I was very excited about pouring my life into this new ministry as I had been teaching for approximately ten years and felt that I had the necessary experience in helping to build this school. I always gave my best and went above and beyond what was expected of me. I moved forward in acquiring certification with the association within the denomination of that schools affiliation. However, as time went on, it seemed that any suggestions I made were not appreciated or accepted by some of the leadership of the school. Each year that I stayed became more challenging, and I prayed that God would just release me by opening the next door.

I stayed very frustrated during this time of my life. Instead of allowing God's peace to rule my heart, I allowed circumstances and other people's actions to control my emotions. Many times in life we think that our frustration is about the other person, but that which angers us can control us if we let it. Due to all of this inner turmoil, I continually prayed for God to open the next door and let me move on. As each academic year rolled around and it came time to sign a new contract, God did not release me and, therefore, He was telling me, "No!"

Several years into the assignment, God dealt with my heart and let me know that regardless of the circumstances that surrounded me, I needed to learn to have joy. He had told me this through the lady in our former congregation, but somehow I refused to connect the two.

You may question whether joy is a choice or not. Through the word of God, I see that joy is a choice, and it comes when we relinquish our grip on the situation we are facing and trust God to work it out as He sees fit. We exert so much energy both mentally, physically and even spiritually when we struggle in the situation that God has orchestrated to fine tune areas of our life that are not producing the qualities He desires. When we rest in Him we will truly find that "the joy of the Lord is your strength" (Nehemiah 8:10). When we recognize that we are to have joy in the hardships, we can have peace in our hearts when the storm is raging around us. First Chronicles 16:27 says, "Splendor and majesty are before him; strength and joy are in his dwelling place." Therefore, resting in Him is essential while we are facing life's difficulties. James 1:2-3 says, "Consider it pure joy, my brothers and sisters, whenever you face trials of many kinds, because you know that the testing of your faith produces perseverance." That perseverance is needed if we are to finish the race.

A lesson can be learned from the eagle that parallels with storms we face in life. The eagle knows that a storm is coming long before it breaks. It is then that the eagle will fly to the highest spot it can find, and wait for the winds to come. "When the storm hits, it sets its wings so that the wind will pick it up and lift it above the storm. While the storm rages below, the eagle is soaring above it. The eagle does not escape the storm. It simply uses the storm to lift it higher. It rises on the winds that bring the storm."[v] Do you see the parallel here between the eagle and us as we face spiritual storms? God desires us to rest in Him as we ride out the storm. He wants us to soar above it, not be weighted down by it.

During this difficult season of my life there was a song that pulled me through entitled "You Are" by Ron Kenoly.

You are the love of my life;
You are the hope that I cling to.
You mean more than this world to me.
I wouldn't trade You for silver or gold;
wouldn't trade You for riches untold.
You are, You are my everything.

I wouldn't take one step without You;
I could never go on.
I couldn't live one day without You,

'cause I don't have the strength
to make it on my own.[vi]

Once I learned the lesson that God desired, He opened the door for me to move on to the next assignment. Through the situations that God sent my way, I learned to have joy as I learned to yield the situation to Him. As I look back and reflect upon that time there were many other areas of my life that God dealt with during those years to help me along the journey of life. As Christians we often criticize the Jewish nation (Israelites) for wandering in the wilderness for forty years, but I know that I have made a few extra laps that were probably unnecessary and repetitive in my own life due to my lack of letting go and letting God take control of the situation.

Many times I have grown restless in situations that I was praying about, and I wanted to bail out in the middle of it. The waiting time is tough! Waiting tests our patience, integrity, and character. However, that is when those qualities are being developed in our life. This is also the time when trust is being forged; trusting that God will work out every detail for His glory. It may not be the way we want it, but we have to remember that "no" is an answer. We may not like it because many times we can be selfish and want things our way. The truth be known, we probably can justify in our minds why we have every right to bail out and take matters into our own hands. However, when we give our life to Christ we must forsake our rights and follow His will to the point of daily laying down our lives.

If God says "no" then there is a reason, and I have come to learn that the next thing God does will be better than the last thing He did. There will be times in our life when well-meaning Christians, friends, and family members will not even understand why we are not moving forward and acting on a situation. When we look at the outcome through the natural (commonsense) lens, it all makes sense and would seemingly bring us peace and joy; maybe even instant gratification. However, good is the enemy to best, and we have to trust that God's ways are not our ways. When we have heard from God, then we need to be patient and trust Him to work everything out on our behalf and in His time. We cannot allow ourselves to doubt in the dark what He showed us in the light.

~ 11 ~

Living by Faith

*"And my God will meet all your needs
according to the riches of His
glory in Christ Jesus."*
Philippians 4:19

Many who have served the Lord for any length of time have sung the hymn "Living by Faith" countless times, but do we really live out the words that we sing? In the last part of the first verse it says, "all of my worry is vain."[vii] I recently read somewhere that only eight percent of what we worry about ever comes to pass. Therefore, that only stands to confirm why God instructs us not to worry. Worry gives us a lot of heartache and produces nothing that is profitable. Matthew 6:25 says, "…do not worry

105

about your life, what you will eat or drink; or about your body, what you will wear." To wrap up His thoughts on the matter Christ says "But seek first his kingdom and his righteousness, and all these things will be given to you as well" (Matthew 6:33).

After twenty-some years of ministry God led my husband and me to resign the church we were pastoring, but He did not immediately show us the next door to walk through. As we stepped out in faith, we thought that we would go through a short sabbatical. Six days into the sabbatical, as I was going about my Saturday routine of cleaning the house, I began to try to find a place for insurance policies and important papers that were accumulating on the desk. As I was working on this project I also decided to go through some other items that I had not used in a while. About four years prior, my brother and his wife had given me a journal and address book for my fortieth birthday. I had written in the journal on several occasions, but never even opened the address book as I had one that I was currently using. My thoughts were that I could re-gift the address book or share it with someone who could put it to good use. As I opened it for the first time, I discovered a piece of paper that was paper clipped to a page with the following message written on it.

> Lord, where do I go from here? How my heart aches to see my strong, gifted husband reduced to confusion and dependence. He has been a well-respected leader, important to so many people in our family, the church, and community. Please spare him pain and humiliation. Please give me wisdom day-by-day to be the wife I need to be to keep his life happy and productive. I don't know what the future holds, but I know You have promised to be with us both. Thank you for that promise Lord.
> I'm depending on it.[viii]

Even though we both felt this to be God's divine timing to leave his present position as Senior Pastor, we eagerly waited for God to open the next door, but God remained silent. If you have never gone through a transition like this, then I am sure you cannot understand the stress that this can put on a marriage. We had stepped out in obedience to God with two children still at home, one in college and one in high school, and we were living on my Christian school teacher salary. This was unchartered territory for us and we had no inclination as to what was next in our lives.

To this day I have no idea how the note got there, and as you can imagine I hurriedly ran outside to share this glorious moment with my husband. As he washed the car, I told him the whole story and how these scripted words on the note were my very thoughts. He began to cry as he told me his deepest thoughts and feelings during this time of waiting. One thing I am certain of is that God allowed me to find the note on that particular Saturday to give me and my husband a ray of hope, and to let us know that He was working all things out for our good, but most of all for His glory; but most of all, how much He really cared for us.

The prayer of my husband's heart through this whole sabbatical was that he would not lose his integrity. I have recently been reading the book by Stormie Omartian, *The Power of a Praying Wife*. I love what she says in the chapter that addresses integrity. She states,

Integrity is not what you *appear* to be when all eyes are on you. It's who you are when no one is looking. It's a level of morality below which you never fall, no matter what's happening around you. It's a high standard of honesty, truthfulness, decency, and honor that is never breached. It's doing for others the way you would want them to do for you. A man of integrity says something and means it. He doesn't play verbal games so you never really know where he stands. He knows to let his "Yes" be "Yes" and his "No" be "No"......He will not play both sides of the fence to please everyone. His goal is to please God and do what is right.[ix]

What wise words for all of us to heed and strive to achieve in our daily lives.

In our time of waiting, do we question if God knows where we are? Even when we question what He is doing, He knows our every thought. He can answer our prayer in a thousand creative ways. God in His foreknowledge knew that on that very day I would take a book that had been given to me four years prior, flip through it, and find a note of encouragement just to get me and my husband through a difficult time of waiting. How the note got there is really not that important to me. What is important is that God knew what I needed at that moment and He supplied it. If He can place a coin in the mouth of a fish for the disciples to pay their taxes, then He can put a note in an unused address book for my encouragement.

As my husband and I discussed what had just happened, we talked about continuing our monthly missions support on my income. The resounding answer from both of us was "yes." Over the years we have trusted God to enable us to give faithfully to missions every month. I will attest that God has blessed our faithfulness, especially during what became a ten-month sabbatical. Through His provision, He faithfully met our needs (See Malachi 3:6-10). I will add that my husband and I have always given liberally to missions, on a monthly basis, above our tithe and offering. The tithe is commanded of God as stated in Leviticus 27:32, "every tenth animal that passes under the shepherd's rod will be holy to the Lord" and Deuteronomy

14:22, "Be sure to set aside a tenth of all that your fields produce each year." It is a tenth of your total income. Offerings are above that and a missions pledge is beyond that.

Many individuals seem to think that tithing is an option. Nowhere in Scripture do I find that to be true. However, I do read what God has to say for those who do not tithe in Malachi 3:6-10. Verses 8-10 of this same chapter are very clear of how God feels about this command when we break covenant with Him; "Will a mere mortal rob God? Yet you rob me. But you ask, 'How are we robbing you?' In tithes and offerings. You are under a curse-your whole nation-because you are robbing me. Bring the whole tithe into the storehouse, that there may be food in my house. Test me in this," says the Lord Almighty, "and see if I will not throw open the floodgates of heaven and pour out so much blessing that there will not be room enough to store it."

When we were first married we followed the prompting of the Holy Spirit and gave $25 a month to missions above and beyond our tithes and offerings. I will say that $25 was a lot for the amount of income that we were making at that time. Over the years, God has laid it upon our hearts to increase that amount many times over. Therefore, we have acted in faith and given in obedience to God. To our amazement, God has always provided for us above and beyond what we could ever think or expect. What we have belongs to Him anyway. We are just asked to be stewards over it.

He truly cares and wants to be so involved in our lives if we only let Him. If He could do miracles while He was on the earth, He can still perform them today. All we have to do is believe. The word of God says, "You do not have, because you do not ask God. When you ask, you do not receive, because you ask with wrong motives, that you may spend what you get on your pleasures" (James 4:2-3). Whatever you are going through today, maybe you need to ask God specifically for direction in your life.

What are you waiting on? Do you need for God to give you an assurance of "I'm here; I care; I've got it all under control?" Whatever you need today, God cares about every detail in your life and He desires to be a part of it if you will only ask Him.

~ 12 ~

The Middle of a Miracle

*"For the eyes of the Lord range throughout the
earth to strengthen those whose hearts
are fully committed to Him."*
2 Chronicles 16:9

As I mentioned in the previous chapter, God had led my husband to resign the church we had pastored for almost seven years. During this time of waiting, orchestrated by the leading of the Holy Spirit, well-meaning Christians began to ask a plethora of questions. Many of the people and the questions were not encouraging; therefore, we felt that we had to defend what God was speaking to our hearts and doing in our lives. As I study the scriptures, Jesus entered his earthly ministry at thirty years of age and ended it at thirty-three. During those three years, Jesus withdrew from the crowds to spend time alone with His heavenly Father. He showed us by example that a sabbatical is needed from time-to-time. Christ, by His very example, showed us how to live Godly in a sinful world. If Jesus needed times of refreshing and getting alone with His heavenly Father to pray and retreat, how much more do you and I need this in the day and age that we live?

The hardest place to be is the middle of a miracle. It is during those times that we cannot see what God is doing. Many times when He is the quietest He is doing the greatest work on our behalf. Trusting God to make a roadway in the wilderness can be trying and taxing, because we are embarking on new territory. We know that the next thing He does will be better than the last thing He did, *if* we are willing to be obedient and follow in His footsteps. The large lesson in life is learning to cast our cares on Him and leave them there. Many times we want to pick them up and try to work everything out on our own. The circumstances in life are not always easy nor are they what we signed up for, but God allows situations and/or circumstances to come into our lives to draw us closer to Him. We know from the example that Paul lived out in scripture that if we suffer with Christ we will one day reign with Him as well. Philippians 1:29 tells us, "For it has been granted to you on behalf of Christ not only to believe on him, but also to suffer for him." That goes against many Christian's belief systems and comfort zones.

As we go through life we can look at nature and learn valuable lessons; for example, take the Chinese bamboo tree. It is planted in the ground; it is watered and fertilized at the right times. This is done for three years and then somewhere during the fourth year the farmer begins to see a little sprout. Within six weeks the tree has grown ninety feet tall. During that time when there appears to be no growth on the surface, the root system is being formed and prepared for the tremendous growth that will take place in the fourth year. At that time it is ready to harvest.

"Life is much akin to the growing process of the Chinese bamboo tree. It is often discouraging. We seemingly do things right, and nothing happens, but for those who do things right and are not discouraged and are persistent, things will happen. Finally, we begin to receive the rewards."[x]

Many times our Christian walk is the same way. During the times of waiting, God is working things out that we cannot see. In the process, we have to be patient and trust that what He is doing will be the perfect fit for our lives. And in the suffering process we must remember that He will not put on us more than we can bear.

During this time that my husband and I were waiting for God to open the next door, I heard the song "Made Me Glad" sung in church one Sunday morning. The words of this worship song pierced my heart so much that all I could do was weep in the presence of God. I could not even sing that day as God ministered to me and touched my heart as only He can do. This powerful song written by Miriam Webster is still my favorite worship chorus with a message that helped me remain strong through a difficult time in my life. It is truly the love song of my heart to my Savior, Redeemer, and King – Jesus Christ. If I am driving in the car by myself, I love to open the sunroof, crank up the volume and sing this song unto God.

I will bless the Lord forever
I will trust Him at all times
He has delivered me from all fear
He has set my feet upon a rock
I will not be moved
And I'll say of the Lord

You are my Shield, my Strength
My Portion, Deliverer
My Shelter, Strong tower
My very present help in time of need

Whom have I in heaven but You
There's none I desire beside You
You have made me glad
And I'll say of the Lord

You are my Shield, my Strength
My Portion, Deliverer
My Shelter, Strong tower
My very present help in time of need.[xi]

So, what are you waiting for God to do? What are you praying about? What promises has God made to you? Have you been waiting for years for it to come to pass? Do not despise the waiting or germination process in your life. God is actively at work even though you cannot see it with your natural eyes. This is where your faith and patience are tested. Think on these words in Hebrews 11:1, "Now faith is confidence in what we hope for and assurance about what we do not see." Many times we pray and see no visible results, but God is creatively working on our behalf, and we need to thank Him for that. Thanking Him in advance is true faith in action.

Let me encourage you to not curse the darkness while you are waiting. There are things that God wants to show you and teach you during this time. I also encourage you to make journaling a daily discipline. You will be amazed to see God's hand at work in your life. It will also prove to be a great testimony to others as you can reflect back on what God has done in your life.

During the ten month sabbatical, various doors opened for my husband, but neither of us had the peace of God to walk through them. Several of the doors that opened would have provided lucrative positions for my husband and our family. One in particular was a position that others would have sought and probably taken in a heartbeat because it appeared to be a prestigious position. However, prestige does not guarantee the will of God. Therefore, we continued to wait on His leading and the peace of God to direct us.

There were days when emotionally I was up and my husband was down. On other days the scenario was reversed. On the days when we were both discouraged, God used our two children to encourage us and remind us of God's faithfulness to us in the past. How I thank God for blessing us with children who have chosen to follow Christ and have been used many times to encourage us along the pathway of life.

Behind the Scenes

"Eye hath not seen, nor ear heard, neither have entered into the heart of man, the things which God hath prepared for them that love Him."

1 Corinthians 2:9(KJV)

*M*ost of us by nature are not patient people. The waiting time is not fun. We live in an instant society where most things can be acquired with the push of a button. As a result "anticipation" has almost become a thing of the past. It is interesting that God, who spoke this world into existence, does not seem to work from that perspective in our lives. At times He seems to be a crock-pot God in a microwave society. When He does not move or work within our time table we get frustrated, and sometimes we take matters into our own hands.

As I have stated several times throughout the book, when we get ahead of God or take matters into our own hands we mess up what He is trying to do, and accomplish in and through our lives. On the other hand, there are times when we have to be patient. We prayerfully seek His will, and wait for Him to work on our behalf. At His appointed time He comes through, and we may instantly see or eventually see that the results were worth the wait. This has been the case many times as I have sought God's direction to meet needs, and answer prayers in my life. Through previous experiences I knew that God was working, but when circumstances did not change then doubt and unbelief tried to overtake me. If God knows us better than we know ourselves, then He truly knows what is best for us, and how to bring everything to pass in our lives, and when to open the next door.

God honors faith and obedience. Think how you feel when your child obeys you out of love and respect; from a submissive heart. As a parent, it's that proud feeling that sends a smile across your face and fills your heart with joy. I think God must feel the same way when we are obedient to Him. Just as we desire to bless our children, He wants to bless us as well. We forget that He is a personal God, and He desires to bless us more than we want to be blessed.

As a result of those times of testing, and waiting for God to direct our steps, and open the next door I would like to share some of the experiences that came out of waiting on God. He was definitely working "behind the scenes" preparing something special and unique that would meet our needs, and answer a prayer on our behalf. During the times of waiting, my husband and I made a concerted effort to praise God in the midst of our circumstances.

The year was 1985, about eighteen months before we accepted our first senior pastorate position. God was working behind the scenes, and our first house was being built in another state and we were not even aware of it. Up to that time, we lived in parsonages at the churches where my husband served as the Associate Pastor. Another couple had contracted to have the house built, and when it came time to purchase the house their loan did not go through. The house had been sitting empty and the builder was losing money each month that the house remained vacant. Remember, all of this was taking place while we lived and pastored in another state. Being led of the Lord we contacted the District Superintendent and expressed our desire to go to a particular city in that district and pastor. To make a long story short, God opened the door for us to candidate for a church that very weekend and we were invited to a church, in that city, and were voted in as the senior pastor. As a result, we had two weeks to find a place to live. We made two trips back down to the area, and kept coming up empty-handed. At the end of our last visit, the week before we were scheduled to move, I saw a small article in the paper stating that first time home buyers could own their own house with a low down payment and low monthly payments. Nothing else was working at this point, and we were running out of time so I told my husband "What have we got to lose?"

We made a phone call, and met a representative at the house. Please realize that we had been praying about this whole situation for approximately eighteen months, and let me add that God does not do anything half way. We just had to trust Him to work out every detail as He revealed it to us. As soon as we stepped inside the house we looked at each other, and the biggest peace just engulfed us. We both said simultaneously, "This is the house." We told the representative we wanted to buy the house, and he said, "Do you want to see the rest of the house? We said, "That's fine, if you want to show it to us but this is the house."

We proceeded to move forward. To do so we agreed to lease the house so we could move in the following week. They agreed to lease the house until we could be approved to purchase the home. The owner wanted to regain his losses by charging us an exuberant amount each month. We declined that offer but told him that we would be willing to pay his monthly payment to the bank until our loan went through. He accepted our proposal, and we were able to lease the home until our loan was approved six months later.

We later found out that the representative who showed us the house was a Christian, and he was instrumental in helping us save additional money with utility deposits since we were leasing to purchase the home. I would like to tell you that it was easy acquiring our first loan but it had its challenges. There were a few moments when we thought we would not be able to purchase the home as there were setbacks along the way. However, we continued to believe God to work it all out. We were able to move through all of the difficulties due to having an excellent credit record, and that was home for us the next six years. I will add that we could not have chosen a house that was better suited for our needs. Little did we know that while we were praying about the next door to open, God was having a house built just for us 300 miles away in another state.

Let me fast forward about eighteen years and share another testimony of God's faithfulness in our lives. Not only does He supply our needs but many times He gives us the desires of our hearts as well. It was the winter of 2004, several months before God directed my husband to resign the church we were pastoring. I wanted to hire a photographer and have family pictures made at a certain picturesque lake in town. I knew that this endeavor would be quite expensive but wanted to get it done since our children were getting older and I did not know what God had in store for their futures. Now that my husband had resigned the church and was not working full-time I would just have to put this desire on hold or forget about it all together.

Being a school teacher I had the privilege of building close relationships with the parents of the students I taught. In August of 2005 I met with the parents of the students that I would teach during that academic year on Orientation night. As the meeting came to an end, one of the parents approached me and said, "If you would ever like to have some pictures made, just let me know." I smiled and said, "Thanks," and continued to speak with the parents as they left my classroom.

After we had settled in to several months of school I asked this parent if she was serious about taking some pictures and how much would it cost? She responded by saying, "Yes, I am serious, and I want to do it for you as a thank you for teaching my son." Wow! I could hardly believe it since she was a professional photographer. We sent notes back and forth in her son's folder trying to secure a date that would work with her schedule, and our family's schedule. We finally secured a date at the beginning of October and she sent me a note that said, "Oh, by the way, I only take outside pictures at Hollis Gardens." What, I could not believe my ears! That is the exact spot that I wanted the whole time. How could she have known that this was a desire of my heart? Of course she did not know, God knew, and He was using her to fulfill a desire of my heart.

The Saturday before we were scheduled to take the pictures I was thanking God for this answered prayer. While I was praying, and preparing for the day, God spoke to my heart and said, "If I'm big enough to give you a desire of your heart, I'm more than able to work out the details of your husband's ministry." This was during the time of my husband's ten month sabbatical that I mentioned earlier. I just began to weep, and thank God that He cares about everything that concerns us. He wants to be involved in the big and little things of life if we will only take our hands off of the situation and let Him have full control.

The pictures were taken, and she had them developed. She called me to her home to view the pictures. She handed me the bundle of photographs as we walked to my car and said, "By the way, pick out your favorite one. I am going to have it enlarged, and professionally framed for your Christmas present." Today that family portrait is the focal point above our mantle in the family room. The remaining pictures are secured in an album and the testimony that I just shared with you is the first thing that people read as they look through the album. Every person that hears this story is truly touched by God's goodness, and faithfulness.

When it comes to personal finances, my husband and I have always tried to use wisdom and be good stewards of everything that God has entrusted to us. We both hate debt, and will do anything we can to pay off a loan, or bill as quickly as possible. I am very thankful for this discipline in our lives, as many marital problems stem from financial disagreements. In our thirty years of marriage we have never had a misunderstanding or argument about money or finances. Simply put, if we do not have the money for it, we do not buy it. When it comes to big purchases (homes, cars) we pray about God's timing and direction and then pay them off as quickly as possible.

It was the spring of 2006, and we had just completed a ten month sabbatical, that God had led us through. We did not realize that God was getting ready to bless us in a way that we could never imagine. I will add that during this time we continued to give faithfully to our monthly mission's pledge which was above our tithe and offering. The car that I was driving was getting older and had high mileage on it. Due to those circumstances finances were tight as our son was in his senior year of college so we thought we would wait another year to purchase a vehicle. Over a period of several weeks I had been noticing a car sitting at a local credit union on the way to church. I did not think too much about it until one night, on the way home from church I asked my husband if we could stop and look at the car. He said sure; so we looked at it and saw that it was brand new with only 1,300 miles on it, and completed loaded. It was a shiny black car at that. As we got back in the car to drive home my husband said, "Why don't you give the bank a call tomorrow since you're off work and don't offer them more than $20,000." I agreed to that plan and made a list of questions that I needed to ask.

The next morning I called a local dealership and asked the general manager how much that particular car would sell for and she said, "I would not let you have that car for less than $36,000." She proceeded to let me know that I would be foolish not to purchase the car at such a price if we could get if for $20,000. I called the credit union and spoke to the individual who handled the reposed vehicles. I asked him the history of the vehicle, if there was anything wrong with it and what was his bottom figure. He informed me that he was planning on taking the car to the auction in a few hours because it had not sold. I offered him the $20,000 which was $2,000 below what he wanted. He informed me that $20,000 was the price that he would probably get at the auction, so we made an agreement over the phone and settled on that price. I called my husband about the great news and we proceeded to make a trip to the credit union to purchase the car.

As I drove the car home that day it was as if God said to me, "You passed the test and this is my reward for your faithfulness." Now, did God do that with every car we have purchased? No. My husband and I had planned to wait one more year, but God surprised us and blessed us a year early with a brand new vehicle for nearly half the price of what it was valued for. He can do things like that because He is God. I am still enjoying that car seven years later and I would have to say that it has been my favorite car out of all the cars we have owned. I probably would have never thought about purchasing that make and model for myself, but it has proven to be a good vehicle. When God does things, He does them well; far above what we can ask or think of Him.

What are you praying about? What do you need for God to supply in your life? He is the God of more than enough. He cares about every detail of your life. He wants to bless you more than you can imagine. Sometimes we have to take our hands off of the situation and say, "God, here it is. I lay it at your feet. Do with it as you see fit." When we do that we relinquish our control to Him and give Him opportunity to work in our lives.

~ 14 ~

What Do You Do When You're Squeezed?

"But if you suffer for doing good and you endure it, this is commendable before God. To this you were called, because Christ suffered for you, leaving you an example, that you should follow in his steps."
1 Peter 2:20-21

I have never met anyone who likes to suffer; especially for doing good. It is one thing to suffer when we have done something wrong or inappropriate, but suffering because we have obeyed the Lord or chosen the right road seems so unjust. Peter tells us this will happen (1 Peter 2:20-21). As a follower of Christ, we will endure suffering, but God takes notice of it.

Throughout the course of our lifetime we will face stressful and challenging situations. We read in James 1:2-4, "Consider it pure joy, my brothers and sisters, whenever you face trials of many kinds, because you know that the testing of your faith produces perseverance. Let perseverance finish its work so that you may be mature and complete, not lacking anything." Verse 12 of that same chapter adds, "Blessed is the one who perseveres under trial because, having stood the test, that person will receive the crown of life that the Lord has promised to those who love him." The author of this New Testament book was none other than James, the half-brother of Jesus. It was written so that we would know how to live a faithful life in a pressure packed world.

Trials and temptations are inevitable and they are not going to go away. If we do not learn to deal with the tests that come our way, they can be detrimental and even destructive to our health, homes, happiness and hopes. Again James says, "Consider it pure joy.....whenever you face trials of many kinds" (James 1:2).

It has been my experience that many Christians try to avoid trials and tests. They want the blessings of God, but do not want any part of the suffering. God's word says, "If we endure, we will also reign with him" (2 Timothy 2:12). When God's word says to take up your cross daily and follow Him then we must know there will be some pain involved. A cross is used as an instrument of pain and suffering. The crucifixion process, in ancient times, was meant to be a slow torturing death.

When we are in the middle of suffering, how do we count it joy? When we face trying and stressful times, how do we respond? Hard times do not have to defeat nor destroy us. Through these difficult times we need to remain faithful to the word of God and to daily prayer. During these times going to God should be our first resort, but many times it is our last.

The book of Psalms is a great comfort in times of difficulty and suffering. The thirteenth chapter of Psalms addresses adversity head on. Listen to David as he pours out his **complaint** to God. "How long, Lord? Will you forget me forever? How long will you hide your face from me? How long must I wrestle with my thoughts and day after day have sorrow in my heart? How long will my enemy triumph over me?"

(Psalm 13:1-2). From this scripture we can conclude that, in our moment of crisis, it is a normal response to pour out our complaint before God. He is big enough to handle it!

Next the psalmist brings his **request** to God asking Him to act on his behalf. "Look on me and answer, Lord my God. Give light to my eyes, or I will sleep in death, and my enemy will say, 'I have overcome him,' and my foes will rejoice when I fall" (Psalm 13:3-4). Once we have poured out our complaint before God and presented our request to Him, then the Psalmist proceeds to **worship** as he waits and puts his trust in God for the answer. "But I have trust in your unfailing love; my heart rejoices in your salvation. I will sing the Lord's praise, for he has been good to me" (Psalm 13:5-6).

Trials and suffering have a purpose in our lives. God leads us through situations to perfect our faith. He has a greater plan than we can ever imagine. As a Christian our life is on display to a lost and hurting world that needs a personal relationship with Jesus Christ. When the unbeliever has his back against the wall and his world is falling apart, who does he turn to for advice and prayer? Hopefully, he will turn to Christ because of the experience he has seen in you. As a result of watching your life he will see that Christ is his only hope. In turn, he will seek your counsel for direction in life, and you will have an awesome opportunity to minister to him in his time of need.

I have not always had "joy" in the midst of my difficulties for one reason or the other. There have been times that I have not been able to rise above the situation and have joy in spite of the circumstances. When we are cast down, it takes a toll on us physically, emotionally, and spiritually. However, it is so refreshing to be around individuals who have learned how to laugh in the face of adversity; to have joy in the midst of their suffering.

Years ago, I went through a difficult situation that lasted for five years. Before the onset of this difficult time, a lady in our church gave me a word of wisdom and told me that I was getting ready to face some very difficult times, but through it all, God wanted me to learn to have JOY. Sure enough, just as she had said, I began a new teaching position and it was a difficult five years. Between my fourth and fifth year, I told God that nothing was going to rob me of my

137

joy. At the end of that year, God finally brought closure to this test. Throughout those five years I did not share what I was going through with many people outside of my family; however, I do recall a gentleman in our church saying to me, "I don't know what changes have taken place in your life, but it shows all over your face." He had been away from the church for six months and had just returned to Florida for the winter months. I was shocked! I thought I had hidden my situation from others. Well, apparently not. I guess my face had been telling on me. As a result of this trial, I learned many things about myself, others, and how to truly have joy in my life. I learned that situations, trials, tests, or circumstances do not have to rob me of my joy. God desires all Christians to have joy in spite of the trial, because "the joy of the Lord is your strength" (Nehemiah 8:10).

Notice a few of the verses in Proverbs which reveals the matters of the heart and how they affect our lives: "A heart at peace gives life to the body" (Proverbs 14:30).

"A happy heart makes the face cheerful, but heartache crushes the spirit" (Proverbs 15:13). "The cheerful heart has a continual feast"

(Proverbs 15:15b). "A cheerful heart is good medicine, but a crushed spirit dries up the bones" (Proverbs 17:22).

Oh how I wish I had learned the correct way to be cheerful and to have a merry heart, but I allowed other things to rob me of my joy. This was a valuable lesson that God wanted me to learn. It was during this time of my walk with God that I suffered through some sicknesses. As I focused upon my situation I lost sight of the needs of others around me. I pray that I never allow myself to get caught in that trap again.

Let me pose the question to you, "What do you do when you're squeezed?" As you daily go through life, fulfilling your responsibilities, how do you respond to situations and/or interruptions? Jesus did not respond to interruptions with resentment, instead He saw them as opportunities to help others (see Mark 6:31-46). An important lesson to learn is that people are more important than things. Christ set an example for us in this area by showing compassion for others. "A tongue that brings healing is a tree of life" (Proverbs 15:4), and "A cheerful look brings joy to the heart and good news brings health to the bones" (Proverbs 15:30).

May we learn from Christ's example and show compassion and empathy; speak life to others and bring joy to those who are in need.

Therefore, when we are stressed, pressured, or squeezed, what comes out? Would those around us be drawn to Christ or be pushed away by our response and/or reaction? As we go about our daily tasks, do people smell the fragrance of Jesus or the fragrance of the world? We may think that this is a strange concept. However, look at the word of God in 2 Corinthians 2:14-15, "But thanks be to God, who always leads us as captives in Christ's triumphal procession and uses us to spread the aroma of the knowledge of him everywhere. For we are to God the pleasing aroma of Christ among those who are being saved and those who are perishing."

Maybe you have never thought about it that way before. Do people light up when you walk in the room or are they anxious for you to leave? Are you celebrated or tolerated? Some of this can be connected to our personalities, but ultimately we should be drawing others to Christ, not pushing them away. We should make them hungry for the Christ that lives within us and the relationship that we have cultivated with Him. With that thought in mind, what aroma do you create?

~ 15 ~

Don't Despise Small Beginnings

*"Oh that you would bless me and
enlarge my territory!"*
1 Chronicles 4:10

*I*n a recent chapter (Living by Faith, Chapter 11), I mentioned how God led my husband and I to resign the church we had pastored for seven years. We knew this to be God's plan for our lives and sought His direction for the next door that He desired us to walk through. Different opportunities presented themselves during what became a ten month sabbatical. There was a church within driving distance of our home that contacted my husband. They wanted him to interview for the Senior Pastor position. Without even meeting us they offered him a hefty salary due to his earned degrees and years of pastoral experience. We were pleased and flattered, but did not have the peace of God about this offer; therefore, we kindly turned it down. Turning a salary down might be easy to do when you are employed, but being unemployed and not having the promise of a steady paycheck makes the offer more enticing. However, we learned years ago that $10 dollars in God's will a day goes a lot further than $100 a day out of God's will.

During the sabbatical he was also contacted by the president of a Bible College in Rhode Island to be considered for a Vice President position. We flew to Rhode Island where my husband was interviewed for Vice President of Finance and Operations. Before we made the trip to Rhode Island we knew that this position was not for us, but for some reason we felt that we had to make the trip. I do not have an explanation for that except to say that we had the privilege of meeting some wonderful people. We declined the position and continued to wait and seek God's direction for our lives.

My husband submitted his resume to three other churches during this time and he was highly considered for one of them, but God closed those doors. During the sabbatical he wrote the book *"Committed to the Call"* which God laid on his heart to do. It is a practical insight to the ups and downs of ministry. It is also a testimony of God's faithfulness in our lives as we have remained faithful to His calling. Everyone that has read it says that it is a must read for anyone who is entering the ministry, in the ministry, leaving the ministry or sitting on the church pew. He also held evangelistic meetings throughout that summer and taught in the theology department of a local Christian University.

After ten months of waiting on God's leading and direction, the door opened for us to take a church of eighteen people in the city where we resided. We did not seek them out, but through a series of events, they called us to see if my husband was still interested in pastoring. He told them "yes" and they asked if he would submit a resume. After my husband met with the pulpit committee and church board, we were voted in 100%. An important point that I would like to share is that God had directed my husband to go on a fast prior to the invitation. On the thirteenth day of the fast, God specifically spoke to my husband about taking this church. Shortly after the completion of the fast someone from the pulpit committee contacted him about sending his resume'. Some people might say that is a coincidence. Well, my husband often says, "When I pray coincidence's happen. When I do not pray, they do not happen."

Many individuals would have allowed this opportunity to pass them by due to the size of the congregation, the condition of the building and the lack of salary being offered. However, we learned years ago that it is better to obey God than man. The salary that the church offered my husband was minimal to say the least; therefore, he continued to subsidize his salary with adjunct work at the local university. As he preached the Word, encouraged the church to give to missions, loved the people, and worked on improving the building, we began to see the church grow in quality and quantity. As we did everything we could in the natural, beautiful things began to happen. God confirmed His word with salvations, He daily added to the church through members joining the church, and He opened doors of ministry as the congregation stepped out in faith.

Almost seven years later we are conducting two Sunday morning services with an average of 350 to 375 attending each week. The doors are open Monday through Friday for prayer at 7:00 A.M. Over two years ago we purchased twenty-six acres of land and are looking forward to building a new building as the church is growing at a steady pace. We believe for God to supply the finances to pay off the land quickly and build the new sanctuary debt free. It is the church's desire to continue to have the finances to do ministry and support missions simultaneously, yet not be strapped down with a mortgage and debt load. You might be saying dream on, but with God all things are possible.

Every week I stand amazed at what God continues to do in the lives of the individuals God has called us to pastor. I also look out at the collection of faces each Sunday that make up the congregation. They are from all nations, races, and ages. To me, this is a true testimony of a healthy church. On Easter Sunday this year we had 100 attend the Sunrise Service and 448 for the morning Worship service. That may not sound like a lot to you, but from eighteen people six years ago; I praise God for each and every one. We were told by those that have been with the church for many years that this was a record setting number for the church. Are we just interested in numbers for numbers sake? No, but numbers tell you that something is happening, and for that, we give God the glory.

People repeatedly ask, "What is the secret to growing a church?" The design for church building is set forth in the book of Acts. It is saturated in prayer, the Word of God, and people with a mind and vision to work. We believe in the Great Commission that God gave in Matthew 28:19-20, to go forth into the entire world and preach the gospel. This is done locally, as well as through our missions outreach. We currently, financially, and prayerfully, support over sixty-nine missionaries a month, as well as local outreaches within the community.

My husband recently received a letter from the Missions Department of our fellowship with the following statistics concerning our church. Out of 9,000 churches in our fellowship that support missionaries, our church ranks number

479 in yearly giving. We also ranked number 277 in increased giving this past year to missions. Do I share all of this to bring glory to my husband or our church? Absolutely not! I want to proclaim that if God can do it for our church; He can do it for all churches. God is no respecter of persons. What He has done in our church, He can duplicate anywhere. My purpose for sharing all of this is to show what God can do with individuals who will yield their lives to Him and allow Him to work through them.

What are you believing God to do in your life? What has He promised you that has not come to pass? He is a God that never changes. He loves you with an everlasting love and wants the best for you.

You may be reading this and saying to yourself, "My day of opportunity is over; I am too old; no one even cares where I am at or what matters to me. I have blown my chances with God," and the list of complaints could go on and on. Well, God does care about you, and He has a unique plan for your life that only you can fulfill. In His time He will reveal His purpose and plan for your life for He is the God who offers second, third, and fourth chances. All you have to do is yield yourself to Him and give Him the opportunity to work in your life. I challenge you to do that today!

~ 16 ~

My Disappointment....
God's Appointment

*"And call upon me in the day of trouble;
I will deliver you, and you will honor me."*
Psalm 50:15

What do you do when your confidence is gone? Who do you put your trust in? Where do you turn? What do you do next? These are the questions that filled my mind during one of my most recent trials. After working for twenty-one years outside of the home as an educator, my life came to a sudden, abrupt stop! Yes, I had mentioned to God that it would be nice to have time off and not always be living life at such a fast pace. Well, be careful what you ask for, because it just might come to pass and you just might get what you asked for.

I never imagined God would answer my prayers the way that He did, but He knows what is best. One day everything was fine in my life and then, abruptly, I was in the middle of a spiritual storm. As a result, I knew it was time for me to resign my teaching position and walk in faith to see the next door that God would open. This was a storm that tested my character and everything that I had worked for all of my life.

During the next nine months I walked through a time of total dependency upon God as I sought His direction for my life. However, during this time, God used Christian friends to strengthen me through prayer and the Word. One of the first scripture verses that a friend texted me early one morning was "Vindicate me, Lord, according to my righteousness, according to my integrity, O Most High" (Psalm 7:8). Notice in the verse it refers to "my righteousness" and "my integrity." In this psalm David was asking God to move on his behalf because he had done nothing wrong. If we stand clean before God according to His righteousness and His word, then He will vindicate us in due time and work all things out for our good and, most of all, for His glory. There were three things that God brought to my attention during this time and admonished me to do: 1) Seek His direction; 2) Keep my mouth shut; and 3) Watch Him work on my behalf.

In my years of serving the Lord, I have found that some of the greatest wounds ever received have come from fellow Christians. Many times these are people that we have trusted and given our confidence to. First Peter 4:12-13 says, "Dear friends, do not be surprised at the fiery ordeal that has come to test you, as though something strange were happening to you. But rejoice inasmuch as you participate in the sufferings of Christ, so that you may be overjoyed when his glory is revealed." It is easy to understand that we would be tested from unbelievers, but a fellow Christian and friend; unthinkable. However, we see that Christ went through the same thing as spoken prophetically by Zechariah in reference to Christ's crucifixion. Zechariah 13:6 says, "The wounds I was given (I received) at the house of my friends." But, through it all, we are commanded to "bless them that curse you, do good to them that hate you, and pray for them which despitefully use you, and persecute you" (Matthew 5:44 KJV). Somehow, through all of this, I knew that God was carrying and sustaining me. There was also a peace that sustained me.

After going through nine months of testing and waiting, I began to give testimony of what God had done in my life. Many individuals in our church said they never knew I was going through anything. What a true testimony that God was my source of strength as He helped me walk out each day by faith. I spent time in His Word and on my knees waiting for the answers and the next direction I was to take for my life. Indeed His grace is and was sufficient through this great test.

When God is the quietest we often think that He is not working or hearing our requests. However, I have learned through the years that many times He is doing great things on our behalf; many times behind the scenes. We tend to want to look at the outward circumstances to judge whether or not He is working. During these times we often respond by questioning Him and feel He has left us all alone to handle things all by ourselves; quite the contrary. Many times we do not realize this until we have gone through the waiting process. David says, "Wait for the Lord; be strong and take heart and wait for the Lord" (Psalm 27:14). Once again, we have to praise Him in expectation of what He is going to do.

Too many individuals jump ahead of God and take matters into their own hands and try to help God out. That is a tragic mistake! In the stillness of the waiting, we need to learn to listen to His voice because many times he says, "Wait and watch me work on your behalf." Through this time He spoke to me primarily through His word. Occasionally He would use others to give me a word of hope or encouragement which strengthened me and helped me get through the day.

During this season of testing the enemy tried to discourage me on a daily basis. At the same time our nation had been hit with a recession. One day I turned on the news only to hear how my state had one of the highest unemployment rates in the nation. Satan jumped on that and told me that no one wanted a woman of my age to work for them, and he would remind me that no one was interested in hiring me either.

However, as I continued to spend time in the Word of God, I was reminded that God had a plan that I knew nothing about.

In my daily devotions He brought my attention to Psalm 92:14-15 which says, "They will still bear fruit in old age, they will stay fresh and green, proclaiming, "The Lord is upright; he is my Rock, and there is no wickedness in him." I also had wonderful Godly friends who encouraged me by praying for me and gave me scriptures that God would direct them to on my behalf. One in particular was Psalm 32:8, "I will instruct you….in the way you should go; I will counsel you with my loving eye on you." I am so thankful for friends that God places in our lives. They have helped to carry me through many difficulties and weather many storms in life.

While I was in this "holding pattern," I prayed that God would allow me to work part-time as I learned the new position, which would develop into full-time. I also desired to have a flexible vacation schedule since that was not afforded to me as a school teacher. Due to my husband and me moving into the empty-nest stage of our lives, I thought it would be great to pick and choose when I would like to go on vacation instead of always taking it in the summer months.

After waiting several months and pursuing every door that presented itself, a former co-worker emailed and told me about a position at the local college that she thought would be a perfect fit for me. I sent a brief email to the Dean of the School of Education stating that I was interested in the position. A few days passed before she responded to my email. However, the day before she contacted me to set up an interview, God gave me this verse during my devotional time; "**Let the morning bring me word** of your unfailing love, for I have put my trust in you. **Show me the way I should go**, for to you I entrust my life" (Psalm 143:8). The bolded words in that verse are the ones that seemed to jump off of the page that morning as I highlighted them and wrote the date beside it in my Bible.

The interview was set for two days before my daughter's wedding. I also had a house full of company from out-of-town, plus all of the last minute arrangements that a wedding can bring to the mother of the bride. However, I learned long ago that when an opportunity presents itself you have to at least "sample the water" to see if this might be the next door that God has for you to walk through.

The interview went well, but I did not hear anything for about a month. I followed up with a phone call one week after the first interview to let them know that I was extremely interested in the job. For the next few weeks the waiting seemed like an eternity. I had to place my total trust in God knowing that He was working all things out for my good and that "no news was good news."

After a month of waiting, I was asked to come in for a second interview. It went well, but as I am prone to do, I left the interview second guessing myself on every answer that I gave. I did not hear back from them for another month, so I figured they had chosen someone else for the position. As a result, I began to contact other places of employment, but those doors were not opening very wide.

About a month after the second interview, I received a phone call. They wanted to let me know that they could not offer me the job for a couple of months as this was a brand new position and the funds would not be available for three more months. I assured them that it was fine and I was very interested in the position. A few more weeks passed when I received a phone call from the dean asking me to come and fill the position part-time for twelve weeks and then move into full-time. This had been the desire of my heart all along, and the only person that knew this was my husband. I was also very uncertain and even fearful that I would not be able to do some of the tasks within this position, but God gave me the following verse which sits on my desk as a daily reminder of God's faithfulness. "Be strong and courageous, and do the work. Do not be afraid or discouraged, for the Lord God, my God is with you. He will not fail you or forsake you" (1 Chronicles 28:20).

All of this took place a little over two years ago, and I am truly blessed to be doing a job that I love and enjoy. Everyone that I work with is such a blessing and encouragement. The work environment is one where everyone truly cares for each other, and there is liberty to share my faith in God.

Many years before this, fourteen to be exact, I had gone through so much with my education and certification that I made this comment to my husband, "Maybe one day God would allow me to work in the area of teacher certification so no one will ever have to go through what I have experienced." I am sure I never thought the door would open and I would be given this opportunity. However, I am living proof that God will do more than we ever dream possible if we commit and submit our lives to Him.

Another desire that I had was to work part-time and then transition into full-time. WOW! Isn't that just like God? Many times we have dreams and desires deeply tucked away in our hearts thinking they will not come to pass. If they are part of His plan for our lives, then in His perfect time they will come to pass.

After I had gone through the nine months of waiting, and returned to work, I began to give testimony of what God had done in my life. A year later I was given the opportunity to share the whole testimony in my Sunday school class. Since that time several individuals that heard the testimony have experienced similar situations. They both told me that they knew they would get through it because I had walked the same path victoriously. I can truly say that God is the peace speaker to every storm that we face if we can just surrender our insecurity, anxious-ness, restlessness, and worry into His hands. Sometimes He says, "Peace be still" to the storm and sometimes He says "Peace, be still" to us as the storm continues to rage. Either way, God is still in control.

~ 17 ~

BEWARE!

"Guard my life for I am faithful to you;
save your servant who trusts in you.
You are my God;"
Psalm 86:2

No matter when we give our life to Christ, young, old or middle-aged, Satan has our number. He will do everything he can to defeat us. If we are a child of God we are in a spiritual battle; one that will never end. Satan will not stop combating us until we draw our last breath. If that were not the case, why do we continually hear of well-known leaders who have fallen? We continually hear of those who have served the Lord alongside us and have walked away from what they knew was the truth and have fallen prey to the enemies' devices. It is Satan's plan to rob, kill, and destroy our life and he will not be satisfied until he sees our life, our ministry, and our eternal soul destroyed.

It may sound like an oxymoron but Satan is a good devil. He is good at what he does in a diabolical way. He knows where we are most vulnerable, what our vices are, and that is where he usually attacks. Any child of God should be on the Devil's "Most Wanted List." To the extent that we decide to make a commitment to following God's will, then Satan will load up his heaviest artillery against us. He comes along when we least expect it, when we are being mightily used of God and even after a great victory in our lives. Many times this is when we are most vulnerable, because we have just passed another spiritual test, and we have relaxed our guard so we can gather our strength and regroup for the next battle or trial that we will face.

None of us are above reproach, and we never reach a point in our Christian walk where we are immune from temptation. We must always beware of the enemy's tactics and devices. In our time of temptation and weakness, he wants to convince us that God is holding out. He also feeds us a personal lie that sounds something like this, "If God really loved you, He would not allow you to suffer like you are suffering. If He is such a loving God, then He would give you everything you have ever desired and prayed for. Look at the sacrifices you have made for Him and the Kingdom of God." In our times of doubt and suffering, all of these thoughts continually replay in our mind, and these are the times when may ask the question, "Does God even care?"

When we are hurting and vulnerable, it is so easy to fall prey to Satan's lies. Negative and false emotions cause us to think incorrectly and irrationally. That is why we have to daily keep ourselves grounded in prayer and renew our minds in the Word of God; for this is where the battle is fought; in our minds. Many times we know God is for us, and there are scriptures to back it up but our emotions are powerful, and they tend to override what we know. We also know that God loves us, but when we are hurting emotionally our feelings tend to overrule everything. This is when we have to trust God more than our emotions. We must also allow our faith in God to precede our emotions.

God, as a loving father, wants what is best for us. He desires us to be happy, but many times our requests are not in His best interest for us. Just as loving parents do not always give their child what they cry and beg for; God often responds the same way.

You may be praying about a situation that you do not think will ever change. You may have been told by someone you love that things will never be the way you want them or desire them to be. Proverbs 13:12 says, "Hope deferred makes the heart sick." Talk about feeling defeated. When everything we have committed our life too and put our trust in seems to be lost; where do we go and what do we do? When we hit a brick wall or end up at a dead-end street many times that is when God has the opportunity to do a great miracle in our lives.

I believe that God allows every part of us to be tested; our body, soul, and spirit. Through these times it causes an unsettling within us; a time of seeing where our allegiance is. Do we truly give God every part of our life; our mind, our will, and our emotions? It is amazing that during these times one little thought can bring back a plethora of emotions and feelings. If we choose to think on what we do not have or we have waited a lifetime for God to answer our prayer then it leaves us feeling that God is holding out on us. As a result, we may doubt His ability to work in our lives. It is then that we can become angry, defensive, and deeply unsatisfied with life, relationships, and even God. It is here that we must make a choice. We can choose to think negative thoughts and stay cast down, or we can fix our gaze above the situation and begin to praise God in spite of the circumstances. Many times we refuse and resist working with God because the process can be messy and complicated. It is like peeling away the layers of an onion and there are plenty of tears involved with that process. However, God can take ugly situations and build lovely things from them.

Adversity has the potential to build character. Dr. Martin Luther King, Jr. said it well, "The ultimate measure of a man is not where he stands in moments of comfort and convenience, but where he stands at times of challenge and controversy."[xii] The Apostle Paul faced adversity many times in his life, but in one instance he prayed three times for the thorn to be removed. However God's response to him in 2 Corinthians 12:6-10 was, "My grace is sufficient for you, for my power is made perfect in weakness." Upon God's response to his request, Paul says, "Therefore, I will boast all the more gladly about my weaknesses, so that Christ's power may rest on me." That is why Paul could say, "For Christ's sake, I delight in weaknesses, in insults, in hardships, in persecutions, in difficulties. For when I am weak, then I am strong."

If we always had sunshine in our lives we would dry up. So it is with nature, it takes the rain to replenish and nourish the earth so that life can come forth. It is the same in our spiritual lives; we need a balance of sunshine and rain. A popular quote from Vivian Greene says, "Life's not about waiting for the storm to pass; it's about learning to dance in the rain!"

Some people run from adversity and try to avoid it, but without it there can be no growth. You do not get a pearl without resistance and you do not get a diamond without time and pressure. When we accept the adversity that comes our way, realizing that it has purpose, we can trust that God is going to walk with us. We will grow stronger in our faith and knowledge of who He is in the process.

As we walk through trying and difficult times, we must accept that God wants to build our character. When Jesus asked Peter to get out of the boat and come to Him, Peter's faith was maturing. The test of Peter's faith was for something in the future. Just as with Peter, God wants to test our hearts to see what is really in there. He already knows what is there, but He allows the tests and trials to come our way to prove what is in our hearts. Proverbs 4:23 says, "Above all else, guard your heart, for everything you do flows from it." The test is for us, not God; therefore, in the middle of it we must praise God for who He is, what He has done, and what He will do in the future. Many days that is easier said than done. Remember, God is more interested in our character than our comfort. If we cannot trust Him now, we cannot trust Him in the future.

I strongly recommend that Christians have accountability partners. This needs to be someone of the same sex that you ultimately trust, and you know they have your back and your confidence. Yet at the same time they are not afraid to confront you as a spiritual brother or sister and tell you when you are wrong. They also are there to encourage you and pray with you and for you. Proverbs 12:26 says, "The righteous choose their friends carefully."

Being connected and having strong Christian friends in our life, for support, is one of the reasons why we need to find a great church and be faithful to it. We need the support of one another in the good times and difficult times. In my forty-six years of being a Christian, I have never seen such a time where believers find more reasons for not being faithful to what they know they should be doing. The word of God encourages us to be faithful in prayer, Bible study, and to the house of God. We all must definitely heed these words of caution; for Jesus said, "When I return will I find faith on the earth?"

It does not matter how long we have been serving the Lord, we never reach a place of spiritual maturity where we are unable to "fall from grace." Paul reminded the Corinthian church in the New Testament, "So, if you think you are standing firm, be careful that you do not fall" (1 Corinthians 10:12). Notice that this is not a declarative sentence, ending with a period. An exclamation point is used to indicate intensity in getting the point across.

Every day fellow Christians and unbelievers are watching our actions. They are observing and listening. What will our actions tell them? What will our words reveal about us? Will they hear blessing our cursing from our mouth? I came across this poem the other day in an online devotional, and I think it is a powerful reminder of how we need to live our lives.

You are writing a gospel, a chapter each day.
By things that you do; by things you say.
Others read that gospel, whether
faithless or true!
Say! What is the Gospel According to You?
Someone's watching. Someone's listening.
Say! What is the Gospel according to you?[xiii]

Where you go, what you do, what you say, and sometimes what you wear often advertize what you are. You may be the only Bible that others read, so make sure your walk lines up with your talk. I heard a new version of that saying recently at a friend's funeral and I like it even better. Your audio should match your video.

Storms

"Lord, you are my strength, and my protection.
You are a safe place for me to run
in times of trouble."
Jeremiah 16:19 (NLT)

*L*iving in Florida we have six months of "hurricane season." Weeks before the season begins the weather forecasters begin to admonish the listening audience to prepare by stocking up on the items needed should a hurricane hit the peninsula. If the listener heeds the warning and acts ahead of time, they can be prepared if, and when the storm strikes. Jesus gave the same advice about life when He said, "I have told you these things, so that in me you may have peace. In this world you will have trouble. But take heart! I have overcome the world" (John 16:33).

In a devotional by Mary Southerland entitled "Strength for the Storm" she shares the following:

Life is filled with storms of one kind or another. In the midst of thosestorms, we tend to respond as if God has somehow been caught off guard.The storm makes no sense. We can't explain why terminal illness strikesgodly people. We don't understand how our strongest friends can becomeour fiercest critics. The anguish of a broken marriage or the overwhelmingheartbreak of a prodigal child drives us to doubt God's purpose, plan andprovision. The fear of financial ruin paralyzes us. God understands.The Bible is filled with men and women who were storm survivors—people of God who endured great pain and weathered intense life stormsbecause they chose to follow Him. The Apostle Paul, known for persecutingand murdering Christians, was forever changed when he met Jesus

Christ.While God gave him a life of great power and eternal impact, it was also a lifefilled with great storms. Paul learned to 'patiently' endure the troubles, hardshipsand calamities that came his way (2 Corinthians 6:4, NLT).

Because grain was a precious food source to the Romans, threshing grain wasa natural part of everyday life in ancient Rome. In pictures of early Rome, oneman is always seen stirring up the sheaves while another rides over them in acrude cart equipped with rollers instead of wheels. Sharp stones and rough bitsof iron were attached to these wheels to help separate the husks from the grain. This simple cart was called a *'tribulum'* from which we get our word*'tribulation'*. No Roman ever used his tribulum as a tool of destruction—only refinement. God uses our trials and storms as tools of refinement to build in us endurance. The word *'endure'* comes from two Greek words that when combined, give themeaning *'to remain under.'* It is the capacity to stay under the load, to remain inthe circumstances without running away or looking for the easy way out.

The purpose of every storm is to purify and cultivate endurance. Like Paul,we may sometimes feel as if we are being torn to pieces under the pressure ofcircumstances. But his challenge to the Romans compels us to re-examine ourperspective and response to each storm we face. 'We can rejoice, too, when werun into problems and trials, for we know that they are good for us — they helpus learn to endure. Endurance then develops strength of character in us, andcharacter strengthens our confident expectation of salvation (Romans 5:3-5,NLT). Endurance is never passive. It is the picture of a soldier staying in the heatof the battle under terrible opposition but still pressing forward to gain thevictory.[xiv]

In today's vernacular we would say, "No pain, no gain!" This is true in the natural sense and many times even in our spiritual growth as well.

When life gives us obstacles and things that are not fair, we find a way to rise above them regardless of what the circumstances look like. Many of the obstacles in life cause us to stop, reflect, humble ourselves, prayerfully seek God's direction, and view life from a new perspective that we probably never would have considered any other way. It is at that time that we can optimistically see benefits from everything that we have experienced. Stormie Omartian, author of *The Power of the Praying Wife,* says the following about trials, "Our suffering will seem like nothing compared to the glory of God working in us, if we have the right reactions in the midst of the struggle. 'For I consider that the sufferings of this present time are not worthy to be compared with the glory which shall be revealed in us'"[xv] (Romans 8:18).

So many Christians struggle with finding God's will and purpose for their lives. If we sincerely seek His face, He will lead us daily fulfilling the plan He has significantly orchestrated for our life. Many feel like "God's will" is somewhere out there in the future and they will never find it or they have missed it. On the other hand, many people want to judge God's will by the circumstances of life. That is not an accurate predictor either. Peter was in God's will, in a boat, in a storm. Jonah was running from God's will, in a boat, in a storm. Therefore, we can conclude from this that God sends storms in our life for **correction** as He did with Jonah when he was supposed to go to Nineveh. Whereas He also sends storms for **perfection** as He did when Jesus told Peter to get out of the boat and walk on the water.

In our moments of deepest despair we need to remember not to isolate ourselves from our Christian family, but many times that is what we do as an escape. When we are hurting and have to look up to see the bottom, the enemy wants us to believe that our life and situation is a hopeless cause and that is the worst place to be. He also makes us think that no one else has ever experienced what we are going through and there is no way they could ever understand our pain and disappointment. This is a lie and ploy of the enemy, therefore, you must find someone that you can trust, as well as seek help and support from family, friends, and other Christians. There is no pain or tragedy so great that we cannot get through and overcome.

When storms come we think that all hope is lost and our dreams are shattered. There may be temporary setbacks, but our dreams do not die when tragedies and obstacles come our way; they may simply be delayed and put on hold. Somehow, we have to learn to dream again and dig down deep to find the determination to continue moving forward with God's strength. Listen to the words of Solomon in Proverbs 10:25, "When the storm has swept by, the wicked are gone, but the righteous stand firm forever." In the midst of our storms we can claim this word because our hope and foundation is built upon Jesus Christ.

All of this reminds me so much of the Old Testament story of "Joseph the Dreamer." As a teenager, God gave him a couple of dreams that his family would bow down to him. With excitement he revealed his dreams to his family, but they were not thrilled. In fact, his brothers despised him and began to find a way to get rid of him. They did, or so they thought. Joseph was sold into slavery and his brothers thought they had concealed their sin. When the brothers returned home they convinced their father that an animal had killed him. To help cover their story they presented Joseph's "coat of many colors" to their father, drenched in blood.

As the story continues, Joseph arrived in Egypt, and is purchased by Potiphar. As he works for him, God gives him favor and he is entrusted with all that Potiphar has. In due time, Potiphar's wife continually made advances towards Joseph. When her plan does not come to fruition she turns it against Joseph and accuses him of rape and he lands in prison. Thirteen years later he has matured into a thirty-year-old man with integrity and wisdom. He is called from prison to stand before Pharaoh to interpret his dreams and is given the position to lead the nation of Egypt through a very difficult time of famine. Through the process of his brothers making several trips to purchase food for their families, Joseph privately reveals his identity to his brothers. As a result, his whole family is reunited and moves to Egypt and is spared which ultimately saves a whole nation. Talk about a family reunion. It is here that Joseph speaks the powerful words in scripture, "You intended to harm me, but God intended it for good to accomplish what is now being done, the saving of many lives" (Genesis 50:20).

How many times do we question God when hard times and tragedy comes our way? Do we only desire to serve God when things are great and going well? If we do, we may never discover God's grace, compassion, and mercy that are extended through the difficult times of life. He is truly more than enough for everything that we face. It is through these times that He wants to make us into the men and women of God that He wants us to be. Instead of blaming God, we need to look at it as a new opportunity to see what God has in store for us and know that when we come through on the other side there will be great things in store for us. Plus, we will be able to help others when they go through difficulties as well.

A powerful song by Hillsong United, "Still," goes hand-in-hand with the storms that we face. I believe it is a true declaration of where we need to place ourselves as we ride out the storm.

Hide me now
Under Your wings
Cover me
Within Your mighty hand

When the oceans rise and thunders roar
I will soar with You above the storm
Father you are King over the flood
I will be still and know You are God

Find rest my soul
In Christ alone
Know His power
In quietness and trust

When the oceans rise and thunders roar
I will soar with You above the storm
Father You are king over the flood
I will be still and know You are God.[xvi]

Don't Lose Your Song

"But I will sing of your strength, in the morning I will sing of your love; for you are my fortress, my refuge in times of trouble, You are my strength, I sing praise to you; you, God, are my fortress, my God on whom I can rely."

Psalm 59:16-17

*G*od's word tells us that the joy of the Lord is our strength. As I mentioned at the beginning of the book, music has always encompassed my life from the time I was a small child. Growing up in church surrounded me with great songs of praise and worship unto God. My mother and father have always enjoyed music, and I attribute much of my musical ear to God placing that gift in my life. Sitting next to my mom, in church, I would listen to her sing during church and choir practice. She sang alto, so I trained my ear to hear the harmony as each song was sung. My parents also encouraged me and my brother and sister to play musical instruments and use our talents for the Lord. Therefore, I played the clarinet during middle school and the drums when I was twelve. I sang specials in church with my brother and sister, and eventually sang in a group with my sister and pastor's daughters during my teen years. I also began playing the piano by ear in my later teens and have played the piano at every church we have pastored when needed. This ultimately instilled within me a love for music and singing which remains my first love to this day.

Music is a powerful tool and it is an act of worship as we sing declarations of praise unto God. In the Old Testament when the Israelites where instructed to go forward and conquer new territory, that God said was rightfully theirs, they were instructed at different times to put the musicians and singers out in front of the others. As they obeyed God's instruction, and offered up praise and worship, He ultimately gave them the victory. Remember, praise is to

God what complaining is to the enemy. Many times throughout scripture we are admonished and commanded to praise God not matter what we feel like doing at the moment. I believe many spiritual battles that we go through are won or lost by our sacrificial praise. Praise frustrates the enemy and releases power within the heavenlies where spiritual activity takes place. There are various examples of spiritual warfare referenced in scripture: Daniel 3-4; Revelation 12:7; 2 Corinthians 10:4; Ephesians 6:12; and Luke 4:18, 10:19.

Think of Daniel in the Old Testament. He prayed for twenty-one days. God heard him on the first day, but there were strongholds in the heavenlies between God's mighty angels and Satan's demons. Even though God heard Daniel on day one, he continued to bombard heaven for the answer, praying against and through all of the opposition that was hindering his prayers from being answered.

As an act of obedience we must offer up a sacrifice of praise and thanksgiving unto God; for who He is, what He has done in our lives and what He will do in the future. When God is exalted, Satan's power is diminished. There is nothing like a song in the heart of a saint that brings glory to God and peace in the midst of our suffering and pain. When we offer up praise and exalt the name of Jesus, the enemy fears and trembles, ultimately confusing his plans (see 2 Chronicles 20:21-22). That is why Satan desires to steal our song.

One of the greatest enjoyments for me is singing on the praise team at church. Years ago I was experiencing some medical problems that affected my voice and I was unable to sing. During that time I had to take a sabbatical from the praise team. When each worship service began I would open my mouth, but nothing came out. My heart was broken as I sat on the second row and offered silent worship from my heart unto God with tears streaming down my face. I wanted so desperately for my voice to cooperate, but there was nothing there. Was my song gone? Would I ever be able to sing again? These questions would go through my heart and mind every service as I desperately pleaded with God to heal my voice.

During this time of my life the words to "Heart of Worship (When the Music Fades)" by Matt Redman took on a whole new meaning for me. Knowing the history behind Matt writing this song sheds light as to why it has impacted my life so powerfully during a time when I was unable to sing.

Here is the story as told by David Schrader. *"The song dates back to the late 1990s, born from a period of apathy within Matt's home church, Soul Survivor, in Watford, England. Despite the country's overall contribution to the current worship revival, Redman's congregation was struggling to find meaning in its musical outpouring at the time.*

"There was a dynamic missing, so the pastor did a pretty brave thing," he recalls. "He decided to get rid of the sound system and band for a season, and we gathered together with just our voices. His point was that we'd lost our way in worship, and the way to get back to the heart would be to strip everything away."

Reminding his church family to be producers in worship, not just consumers, the pastor, Mike Pilavachi, asked, "When you come through the doors on a Sunday, what are you bringing as your offering to God?"

Matt says the question initially led to some embarrassing silence, but eventually people broke into a cappella songs and heartfelt prayers, encountering God in a fresh way.

"*Before long, we reintroduced the musicians and sound system, as we'd gained a new perspective that worship is all about Jesus, and He commands a response in the depths of our souls no matter what the circumstance and setting. 'The Heart of Worship' simply describes what occurred.*"[xvii] I have included the lyrics below.

Verse 1

When the music fades
All is stripped away
And I simply come
Longing just to bring
Something that's of worth
That will bless your heart

Bridge

I'll bring You more than a song
For a song in itself
Is not what You have required
You search much deeper within
Through the way things appear
You're looking into my heart

Chorus

I'm coming back to the heart of worship
And it's all about You
It's all about You, Jesus
I'm sorry, Lord, for the thing I've made it
When it's all about You
It's all about You, Jesus

Verse 2

King of endless worth
No one could express
How much you deserve
Though I'm weak and poor
All I have is yours
Every single breath

Bridge
Chorus
Chorus

This song spoke to the deepest recesses of my heart and life.

I learned a valuable lesson during that time. Circumstances and sickness may limit us from doing the things that we love and enjoy; however, it cannot take the song from our hearts.

The scripture tells us "The Lord does not look at the things people look at. People look at the outward appearance, but the Lord looks at the heart" (1 Samuel 16:7b). Nothing in this world can rob us from giving God the praise that He is worthy of. If it does, it is because we allow it.

God does not always call the qualified to His work; He qualifies the called. A great example of this is David who was a shepherd boy tending to his father's sheep when God called him to be the next king of Israel after Saul. The scripture says that Samuel asked Jesse, "'Are these all the sons you have?' 'There is still the youngest,' Jesse answered. 'He is tending the sheep,' Samuel said, 'Send for him; we will not sit down until he arrives.' So he sent for him and had him brought in. He was glowing with health and had a fine appearance and handsome features. Then the Lord said, 'Rise and anoint him; this is the one'" (1 Samuel 16:10-12).

Many times God uses the insignificant ones to accomplish His greatest work. Please do not despise the path God chooses to take us down in life. Many times He takes us through a humbling process – a breaking of our wills so that we can be submitted to His plan and design for our life. I have often found that the way up with God is down. It is in these times that we die to self, and it is here that He makes us into the unique individual that He desires us to be so that we can do a great work for Him.

Throughout every test and obstacle that God has taken me through, it has been my desire to become more like Christ. I believe that each desert experience has been to crucify more of my flesh so that more of His presence can shine through my life. As I continue on this path of life, and endeavor to allow Jesus Christ to be the Lord of every area, there will be more valleys, deserts, and mountains to climb. With Him leading me I trust that others will look at my life and say that I was a reflection of Christ, not just a reflection upon Christ. Don't allow any situation or circumstance to rob you of your joy or the song in your heart, because from God's perspective, "Praise looks good on you!"

Conclusion

hat's next? Only God knows. He is the One who will fill in the lines as life goes along. One thing is for sure; there will be storms, difficulties, challenges and obstacles to continually face, as well as sunshine and times of joy and rejoicing. Whether we are an optimist or a pessimist, it does not matter. Storms will come. How we choose to handle the storms and obstacles that come our way will many times determine the outcome.

Now that we have walked together down some bumpy, rocky, dusty and narrow roads that have made up my life, I trust God's faithfulness has been evident through it all. In myself, this would not have been the life I would have chosen as I never saw myself being a pastor's wife or in full-time ministry; yet this was God's plan for my life. When we give our lives to Christ, it is like signing our name at the bottom of a blank page and letting him fill it in as we go. Although there have been times when the journey has been hard and difficult, God has graciously seen me through it all and meant it for my good. I have learned through experience; when I yield to his leading and do not resist, the ride is not as bumpy. As Psalm 34:19 says, "The righteous person may have many troubles, but the Lord delivers him from them all."

One thing is for certain, we must be prepared to face the challenges that each day brings. Therefore, we must not go into battle unprepared. Each day we have to put on the whole armor of God as Paul spoke about in Ephesians 6:11-17. In 1 Samuel 13:16-22 we see that Saul had assembled the troops against the Philistines. Since a blacksmith could not be found in all of Israel, the men went to the enemy's territory (Philistines) to have their plowshares, mattocks, axes and sickles sharpened. The scriptures say that on the day of battle not a soldier with Saul and Jonathan had a sword or spear in their hand. Only Saul and his son Jonathan had weapons to fight.

We also know that Samson was a man of God who continually dabbled in the enemy's territory, little-by-little giving away the secret of his God-given strength. Only to find that one day his strength was totally gone. He had let his guard down one too many times and he literally got a haircut in the devil's barbershop (Delilah's lap).

Sometimes God allows us to go through test of correction and tests of perfection. If they are tests of correction, then I pray we all learn our lesson the first time and do not repeatedly stay in our pattern of rebellion and resistance to God's plan for our lives. If it is a test of perfection, then may God perfect work be perfected in our lives. Through it we need to pray that God gives us the grace and patience to endure all that He wants to accomplish in our life.

I am sure that each of us has faced our own obstacles that have had unique challenges. Through these experiences there were possibly decisions made that were life changing. Change is not always easy and it is more difficult for some individuals than others; however, it all depends on the way we look at it. Some changes are of our own making and some changes are a result of situations that are beyond our control.

Whatever the reason, we can view it from a positive or negative lens. Many times that view determines our outcome and "life lessons" that will be learned along the way. Ultimately the path can still lead us to the same destination, but one path may have more curves and rocky places than the other.

No matter which path we choose, we have to forge on. Looking back and second guessing our decisions will only distract us from our goal and destination which can create a lot of worry. So, we have to put our trust in Christ and enjoy the journey. Life is not always easy and sometimes it is just plain hard; but remember, the sun is always shining even though the clouds may hide its view. As we move forward let us ask ourselves, "What is it that God may want to teach me about myself and life along this path?" If we view it from that perspective, the journey can become an acceptable challenge knowing that God is in control.

A song that Janet Paschal wrote many years ago, "If I'd Had My Way" holds the message of the way I would have loved my life to be. If life would have always been sunny and easy I would never have grown into the spiritual woman that God designed me to be nor learned about His character.

Throughout the song Janet speaks of choosing the easier way over the difficult. Here are a few of the lines so you can gather the meaning of what I am trying to get across.

If I'd had my way about it, I'd have danced in
grassy fields and fragrant meadows.
And risen in the morning just to hear
the robin's lovely melody.
I'd have rested in wide spaces, high
above the hurting places,
And found a cross that asked much less of me.
Never sailed in raging wind or troubled sea,
if You'd thought it best to leave it up to me.

But if I'd had my way, I might have been
wading through the river
When You wanted me to walk upon the sea.
And if I'd had my say and all of my wants
and whims and wishes,
You knew how weak, how shallow
I would be, If I'd had my way.

However, as the song comes to an end she resolves it all by saying,

> I trust Your wisdom over mine.
> 'Cause You've proven over time
> That in my narrow way of seeing things
> I leave the best behind sometimes.
> I might not have stayed as close if
> I'd had my way.[xviii]

How true this is for many of us that label ourselves as Christian. Scripture tells us we must crucify our flesh daily. However, the flesh dies hard and it is a painful process, but one that is necessary if we are to become all that Christ wants us to be. Piece by piece, God is making a masterpiece out of our lives. No one else has the same pattern or design, as you, because He is the Master Designer and He loves variety.

Through every situation that I have faced, I would go through it again. As I reflect over the circumstances I see how God has worked all of it for my good. Another necessary discipline is to renew our spiritual man in the Word on a daily basis. It is not always easy but necessary for us to grow in Christ. Remember, what we feed will grow and what we starve will die.

As we face challenges and obstacles in life, do not look at them as dead ends or roadblocks, but see them as a mountain to climb so that we might view the beautiful horizon at the peak. Remember an obstacle is placed there to try and hinder your spiritual growth, but cling to this verse in times of hardship, "I can do all things through Him who gives me strength" (Philippians 4:13). If God removed all the obstacles from our lives we would never know Him in His fullness or become all that He desires us to be.

I will close with this quote that I found by Erma Bombeck, "When I stand before God at the end of my life, I would hope that I would not have a single bit of talent left, and could say, 'I used everything you gave me.'"[xix] Lord I pray let it be so. No matter where we are in life, God is our source for everything that we need. If you have never met Him and accepted Him to be the Lord and Savior of your life, you can do that today. If He is your personal Savior and you are struggling or stuck in an area, I trust that God can take the obstacle you are facing and us it to mature you so that you can be victorious in your walk with Him.

Endnotes

Chapter 1
[i]Obstacle, http://dictionary.reference.com/browse/obstacle (April 2012).

Chapter 7
[ii]Marriage Tips, *Unresolved Conflict,* http://marriage.about.com/library/bltip1018.htm (May 2012).

[iii]Steven P. Wickstrom, *Resolving Conflict in Your Marriage,* http://www.spwickstrom.com/conflict/ (June 2012).

[iv]*Divorce Rates in America,* http://marriage101.org/divorce-rates-in-america/ (May 2012).

Chapter 10

[v]*Eagles in a Storm*, http://www.indianchild.
com/eagles_in_a_storm.htm.
(January 2010).

[vi]Ron Kenoly, *You Are*, http://www.lyrics007.
com/Ron%20Kenoly%20Lyrics/You%20
Are%20Lyrics.html
(June 2012).

Chapter 11

[vii]*Living by Faith*, http://www.hymnlyrics.org/
newlyrics_1/living_by_faith.php
(June 2012).

[viii]Author Unknown, personal letter, February
2005.

[ix]Stormie Omartian, *The Power of the Praying Wife*
(Eugene, Oregon: Harvest House Publishers,
1997) 117.

Chapter 12

[x]*Story of Bamboo*, http://bigbamboollc.com/
about/story-of-bamboo/ (June 2012).

[xi]Miriam Webster, *Made Me Glad*, http://www.lyricsfreak.com/h/hillsong/made+me+glad_20542544.html (June 2012).

Chapter 17

[xii]Dr. Martin Luther King, Jr. Quotes, *Brainy Quote,* http://thinkexist.com/quotation/the_ultimate_measure_of_a_man_is_not_where_he/215197.html (January 2013).

[xiii] Sharon Jaynes, *Someone's Watching Someone's Listening,* http://www.girlfriendsingod.com/?s=someone%27s+watching%2C+someone%27s+listening (May 31, 2012).

[xiv]**Chapter 18**
Mary Southerland, *Strength for the Storm* http://www.girlfriendsingod.com/2012/strength-for-the-storm/ (April 2012).

[xv] Stormie Omartian, *The Power of the Praying Wife* (Eugene, Oregon: Harvest House Publishers, 1997) 113.

[xvi]Hillsong United, *Still*, http://www.lyrics-mode.com/lyrics/h/hillsong_united/still.html (June 2012).

Chapter 19
[xvii]Matt Redman, *When the Music Fades*, *http://www.crosswalk.com/church/worship/song-story-matt-redmans-the-heart-of-worship-1253122.html* (April 2012).

Conclusion
[xviii]Janet Paschal, *If I Had My Way About It*, http://philhoover-chicago.blogspot.com/2004/09/if-i-had-my-way-about-it.html (January 2013).

[xix]Erma Bombeck Quotes, Brainy Quote, http://www.brainyquote.com/quotes/authors/e/erma_bombeck.html (January 2013).

Appendix

Chapter 7-*Tough Love*

Willard F. Harley, Jr. *His Needs, Her Needs* (Grand Rapids, MI: Baker Publishing Group, 2011).

Sharon Jaynes, *Becoming the Woman of His Dreams* (Eugene, Oregon: Harvest House Publishers, 2005).

Stormie Omartian, *The Power of the Praying Husband* (Eugene, Oregon: Harvest House Publishers, 2001).

Stormie Omartian, *The Power of the Praying Wife* (Eugene, Oregon: Harvest House Publishers, 1997).

Gary Thomas, *Sacred Marriage* (Grand Rapids, MI: Zondervan, 2000).

CPSIA information can be obtained at www.ICGtesting.com
Printed in the USA
LVOW060505020513

331960LV00001B/1/P